Kaffe Fassett's
QUILTS in BURANO

Designs inspired by a Venetian island

featuring
Liza Prior Lucy
Brandon Mably

The Taunton Press

First published in the USA in 2020 by

The Taunton Press
Inspiration for hands-on living®

The Taunton Press, Inc.
63 South Main Street
Newtown, CT 06470
email: tp@taunton.com

Patchwork designs	Kaffe Fassett, Liza Prior Lucy, Brandon Mably
Quilt making coordination	Heart Space Studios (Janet Haigh, Julie Harvey, Ilaria Padovani)
Technical editor	Bundle Backhouse
Quilting	Judy Irish and Mary-Jane Hutchinson
Designer	Anne Wilson
Art direction/styling	Kaffe Fassett
Location photography	Debbie Patterson
Additional photography	Brandon Mably (pages 6tr, 6cm, 6cr, 6br, 7l, 78, 144)
Stills photography	Steven Wooster
Quilt illustrations	Heart Space Studios
Map illustration	Héloïse Wooster
Publishing consultant	Susan Berry (Berry & Co)

Library of Congress Cataloging-in-Publication Data in progress

ISBN 978-1-64155-119-9

Colour reproduction	XY Digital, London

Printed in China

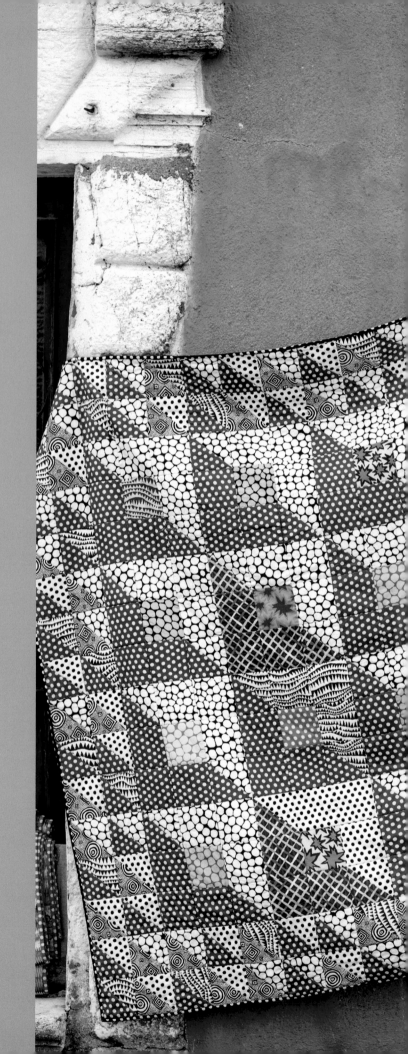

Page 1: My jaunty little *Geometric Snowballs* quilt enlivens a colourful two-tone doorway on this jewel-like island.
Right: The black-and-white background for my *Roman Tiles* quilt was inspired by the white stone surrounds of the doorways and windows of Burano's brilliantly painted houses.

Contents

introduction

What, one wonders, started off the carnival of colours in this charming little island of Burano in the Venetian Lagoon. When most of the Mediterranean villages have a typical assortment of gold, rust, dusty pink and beige buildings, what inspired this island to paint almost every house in saturated, blazing colours found in only a handful of towns in the world?

Whatever it was, I am on my knees thanking the Gods of inspiration for this stunning location in which to show off our quilts. Brandon and I felt like we were on a film set created to delight us with one gorgeous surprising combination after another. We have walked every canal, wandered down every alley and feel we could do at least a dozen different books there. What you see is only what these few pages could afford us to house a selection of our shots and impressions. I, for one, definitely felt I'd died and gone to heaven!

I know that many people are more at home in a monotone world and I, too, find a space furnished in neutral tones very soothing at times. But when I prepare for an exhibition or present my work in a book, I feel a heightened sense of

Fruits of the Forest
by Kaffe Fassett

This quilt with its jewel-like pinwheels reminded me of the gorgeous berry tones of fruits of the forest. See how they glow on this distressed blue wall!

Roman Tiles
by Kaffe Fassett

Just lately I've been having a love affair with black and white in my textile designs. Creating a monotone ground for this quilt was the perfect vehicle into which to drop sharp pastels.

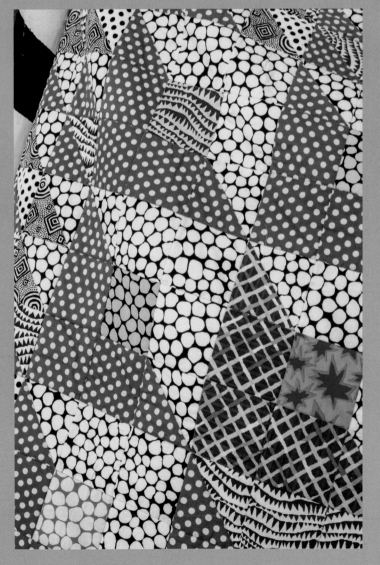

Smouldering Stars
by Kaffe Fassett

There are so many deep rich reds and maroons in our current collection of fabrics that they begged to be brought together. This glowing creation is the result.

theatre is required. So, my search for larger than life colour goes on and occasionally results in something on the scale of this magical toybox.

This is the sort of place I pray we will find, and at last we get to set our quilts in a corner of the world that echoes the colour we find so invigorating. I only hope you feel a fraction of the thrill that we felt every hour we spent on this magical island.

Editor's note: Burano is an island in the Venetian Lagoon, part of the Metropolitan City of Venice, known for its lace work and brightly coloured houses, as well as its ancient church, the Chiesa di San Martino, which has a leaning 17th century bell tower. It can be reached by ferry from Venice. See map on page 144.

Midnight Diamonds
by Kaffe Fassett

This is one of the strongest
of my formats that is ideal
for demonstrating how to
use my large-scale prints.
Loving extremes as I do,
I chose to create this in the
darkest of my current prints.

Ocean Ripples
by Kaffe Fassett

I'm delighted at the way in which blue quilts are coming into focus in the quilt world, so thought I'd go for a good saturated-cobalt effect on this one.

Shimmer Star
by Kaffe Fassett

I've always been drawn to these 'big star' quilts with their ripples of pattern. I went all out on this version, picking wildly contrasting prints and using the jazziest colourway of Brandon's Bali Brocade fabric as a background.

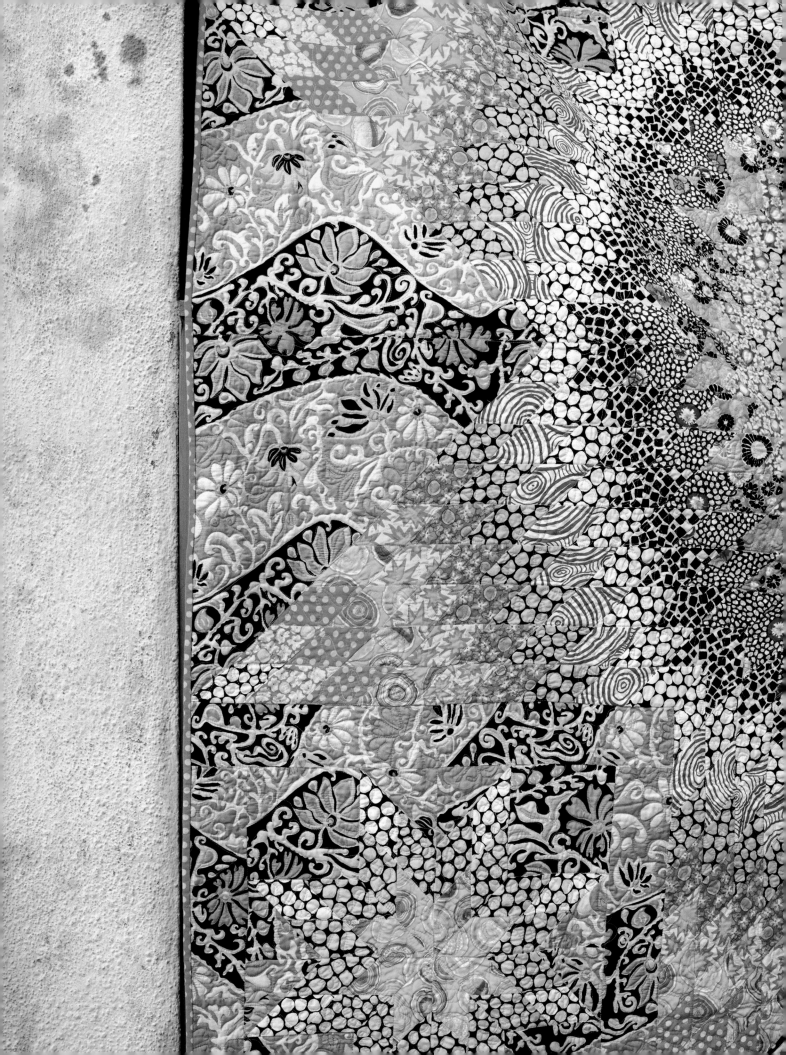

Hot Steps
by Kaffe Fassett

Loved, loved, loved playing with my new Oranges prints and my Promenade Stripes in this dancing technicolour dream of a quilt. Right up my street!

CAMPIELLO DEI SQUERI

Cool Steps
by Kaffe Fassett

Taking all the dusty blues, greens and greys for this cool version of *Hot Steps* (see page 14) gives it such a different look.

OVERLEAF

Tawny Pinwheels
by Kaffe Fassett

Marquetry, with its pictures and motifs in shades of wood tones, has long been a source of fascination. I set out to echo that effect here using Brandon's Bali Brocade fabric in ochre and blue to cool it down.

Dark Garden
by Kaffe Fassett

The use of extreme black
fabrics in this quilt serves
to sharpen the jewel tones.
And it looks so good on the
deeper colours of Burano.

Succulent
by Kaffe Fassett

Coming from California, I grew up loving succulent gardens. This cool green-and-blue toned study reminds me of them.

Honeycomb
by Kaffe Fassett

I borrowed the idea for this from an Indian tie-dyed textile. The warm amber palette echoes it and really pleases me. I think the Sea Urchins backing fabric complements it beautifully.

Flaming Hell
by Kaffe Fassett

All the reds in our fabric collection are great for this easy-to-make quilt. And it is a good way to use large-scale prints. Any colourway can be chosen successfully, as you can see in *Green with Envy* (see page 40).

Framed Log Cabin
by Kaffe Fassett

I loved taking the usually small-scale log cabin block up to this much greater scale and framing all the large-scale prints. This same approach could be taken using any colour palette. I think the Full Blown extra-wide backing fabric is perfect for this quilt.

Sun and Sea
by Liza Prior Lucy

This cheerful quilt of Liza's
has the perfect colouring
for sunny Burano.

Geometric Snowballs
by Kaffe Fassett

Loved taking all my new
Promenade Stripes to make
this small jaunty quilt.
I used black and silver
corners to echo the contrast
of white frames and dark
green shutters of the
windows in Burano.

Green with Envy
by Brandon Mably

With its lively use of greens, Brandon's answer to my *Flaming Hell* (see page 32) quilt offers a very different but equally appealing take on it.

Diamond Carpet
by Kaffe Fassett

I am delighted at the way in which the black and white prints come together with the sky-blue, lavender and pink tones in this jaunty number.

Turkish Coffee
by Liza Prior Lucy

Liza brilliantly uses my
Turkish Delight fabric
to create a wonderfully
rich, dark quilt that has a
distinctly Middle Eastern
feel to it.

shimmer star ***

Kaffe Fassett

This quilt is all about the jazz of contrast prints. I love both the blending and the dramatic breaks in the big central star and how it holds its own on a very strong background. A feature of this quilt is the Bali Brocade fabric used for the backgrounds; when cutting it, you will need to play with it to achieve a flowing design.

SIZE OF FINISHED QUILT
98in x 98in (249cm x 249cm)

FABRICS
Fabrics have been calculated at a maximum width of 40in (102cm), and are cut across the width, unless otherwise stated. Fabrics have been given a number – see Fabric Swatch Diagram for details.

Patchwork Fabrics

JUMBLE
Fabric 1	Rose	¾yd (70cm)
Fabric 2	White	1¼yd (1.2m)
Fabric 3	Gold	1yd (90cm)

CHIPS
Fabric 4	White	¾yd (70cm)

PRIMULAS
Fabric 5	Periwinkle	½yd (45cm)
Fabric 6	Orange	½yd (45cm)
Fabric 7	Pink	¼yd (25cm)

MAD PLAID
Fabric 8	Contrast	¼yd (25cm)

ONION RINGS
Fabric 9	Purple	¾yd (70cm)

BANG
Fabric 10	Yellow	½yd (45cm)

BALI BROCADE
Fabric 11	Contrast	5yd (4.65m)

GEODES
Fabric 12	Gold	¾yd (70cm)

SPOT
Fabric 13	Melon	⅜yd (40cm)

* see also Binding Fabric

ROW FLOWERS
Fabric 14	Contrast	½yd (45cm)

PAPER FANS
Fabric 15	Delft	⅜yd (40cm)

GUINEA FLOWER
Fabric 16	White	⅝yd (60cm)

Backing and Binding Fabrics

LOTUS LEAF
Fabric 17	Lime	9yd (8.2m)

SPOT
Fabric 13	Melon	⅞yd (85cm)

* see also Patchwork Fabrics

Batting
106in x 106in (270cm x 270cm)

FABRIC SWATCH DIAGRAM

Patchwork Fabrics

Fabric 1
JUMBLE
Rose
BM53RO

Fabric 2
JUMBLE
White
BM53WH

Fabric 3
JUMBLE
Gold
BM53GD

Fabric 4
CHIPS
White
BM73WH

Fabric 5
PRIMULAS
Periwinkle
BM71PE

Fabric 6
PRIMULAS
Orange
BM71OR

Fabric 7
PRIMULAS
Pink
BM71PK

Fabric 8
MAD PLAID
Contrast
BM37CN

Fabric 9
ONION RINGS
Purple
BM70PU

Fabric 10
BANG
Yellow
BM72YE

Fabric 11
BALI BROCADE
Contrast
BM69CN

Fabric 12
GEODES
Gold
PJ99GD

Fabric 13
SPOT
Melon
GP70ME

Fabric 14
ROW FLOWERS
Contrast
GP169CN

Fabric 15
PAPER FANS
Delft
GP143DF

Fabric 16
GUINEA FLOWER
White
GP59WH

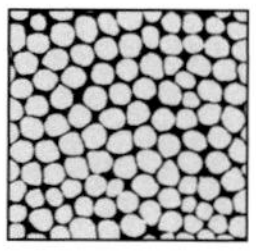

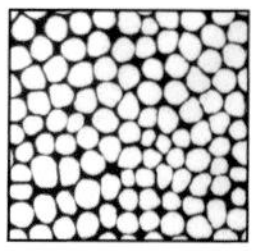

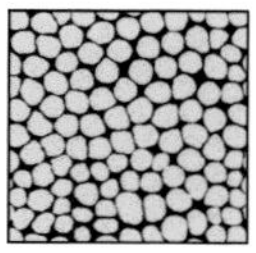

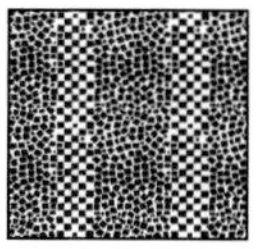

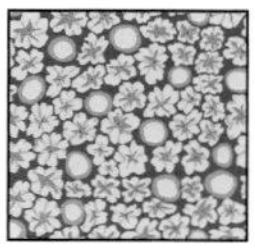

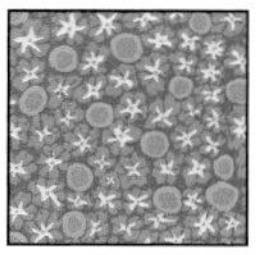

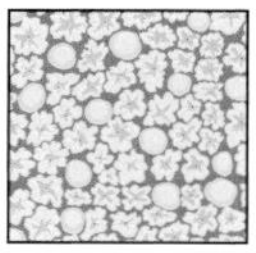

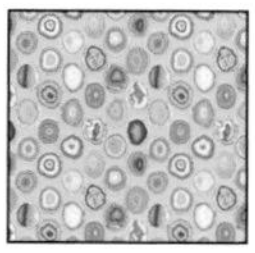

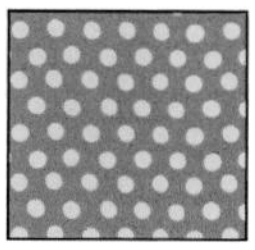

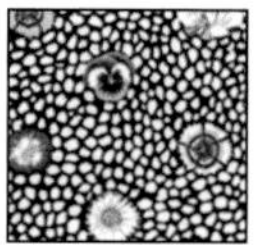

Backing and Binding Fabrics

Fabric 17
LOTUS LEAF
Lime
GP29LM

Fabric 13
SPOT
Melon
GP70ME

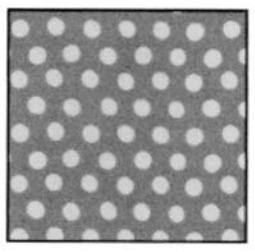

PATCHES

Patches are 45° diamonds cut from 2¾in (7cm) strips.

CUTTING OUT

The centre star is made up of eight points that are sewn together in large diamond-shaped blocks.

Big Central Star

Cut all fabrics for stars into strips 2¾in (7cm) wide from selvedge to selvedge. Referring to the Cutting Diagram, make a 45° cut using the 45° line on your ruler. Cross cut diamonds at 2¾in (7cm). You can cut a minimum of 8 diamonds from each strip. For odd rows use Method 1 and for even rows use Method 2 to ensure bias edges will be matched to straight-grain edges, stabilizing the joined patches.

Cut diamonds from 2¾in (7cm) strips as follows:

Row 1 (Centre) – Fabric 1 (1 strip) 8 diamonds, 1 for each block;
Row 2 – Fabric 8 (2 strips) 16 diamonds, 2 for each block;
Row 3 – Fabric 15 (3 strips) 24 diamonds, 3 for each block;
Row 4 – Fabric 3 (4 strips) 32 diamonds, 4 for each block;
Row 5 – Fabric 5 (5 strips) 40 diamonds, 5 for each block;
Row 6 – Fabric 14 (6 strips) 48 diamonds, 6 for each block;
Row 7 – Fabric 16 (7 strips), 56 diamonds, 7 for each block;
Row 8 – Fabric 4 (8 strips) 64 diamonds, 8 for each block;
Row 9 – Fabric 2 (9 strips) 72 diamonds, 9 for each block;
Row 10 – Fabric 9 (8 strips) 64 diamonds, 8 for each block;
Row 11 – Fabric 1 (7 strips) 56 diamonds, 7 for each block;
Row 12 – Fabric 6 (6 strips) 48 diamonds, 6 for each block;
Row 13 – Fabric 10 (5 strips) 40 diamonds, 5 for each block;
Row 14 – Fabric 12 (4 strips) 32 diamonds, 4 for each block;
Row 15 – Fabric 13 (3 strips) 24 diamonds, 3 for each block;
Row 16 – Fabric 7 (2 strips) 16 diamonds, 2 for each block;
Row 17 – Fabric 2 (1 strip) 8 diamonds, 1 for each block.

CUTTING DIAGRAM

Method 1: Odd rows

Method 2: Even rows

Small Corner Stars

The four small stars, one at each corner, are also made up of 8 points sewn together in small blocks.
Cut diamonds from 2¾in (7cm) strips as follows:
Row 1 – Fabric 12 (4 strips) 32 diamonds, 8 for each small star;
Row 2 – Fabric 3 (8 strips) 64 diamonds, 16 for each small star;
Row 3 – Fabric 2 (4 strips) 32 diamonds, 8 for each small star.

Backgrounds

Fabric 11 is used throughout.

Big Central Star For the side, top and bottom triangles set into the Big Star blocks, with the fabric folded from top to bottom (NOT selvedge to selvedge) so you cut 2 squares at a time, cut a total of 4 squares each 20¾in (52.7cm). Cut squares in half diagonally to make 2 half-square triangles from each, 8 in total.

Small Corner Stars Do not attempt to match the fabric motifs or cut them so the fabric faces in one direction when sewn in place – the background will look better if the motifs face in various directions. Cut 4 strips 6⅞in (17.5cm) wide and cross cut 16 squares 6⅞in (17.5cm). Cut 3 strips 5⅜in (14cm) wide and cross cut 16 squares 5⅜in (14cm). Cut each square in half diagonally, making 2 half-square triangles from each.

BLOCK ASSEMBLY DIAGRAM 1

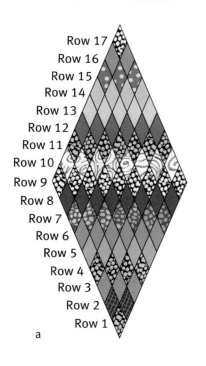

Row 17
Row 16
Row 15
Row 14
Row 13
Row 12
Row 11
Row 10
Row 9
Row 8
Row 7
Row 6
Row 5
Row 4
Row 3
Row 2
Row 1

a

b

BLOCK ASSEMBLY DIAGRAM 2

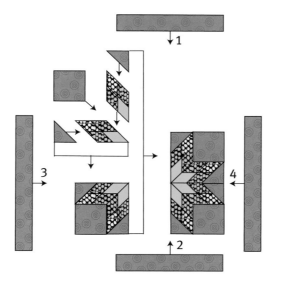

1

3   4

2

Cut 11 strips 4in (10.2cm) wide, trim selvedges and sew together end to end, pressing seams. From this length cut 8 long border strips 4in x 29¼in (10.2cm x 74.3cm) and cut 8 short border strips 4in x 22¼in (10.2cm x 57cm).

Backing
From Fabric 17 cut 3 panels 106in (270cm) long.

Binding
From Fabric 13 cut 11 strips 2½in (6.4cm) wide and sew end to end (see page 141).

MAKING THE BLOCKS
Use a ¼in (6mm) seam allowance throughout.

Big Central Star Blocks
Using the patches cut for each of the eight big-star blocks, arrange the diamonds in 17 rows as in Block Assembly Diagram 1(a). Sew diamonds together in diagonal rows as shown in Block Assembly Diagram 1(b) and press. Press the seams in alternating rows in opposite directions. Sew the diagonal rows together as shown.
Make 8 blocks.

Small Corner Star Blocks
Each small corner star block measures 28¹¹⁄₁₆in (72.9cm) square (finished size excluding seam allowance). Using the small

corner star patches, sew the diamonds together in diagonal rows of 2, then press and sew the 2 rows together.

Lay out the star and the background pieces and sew together in sequence, quarter by quarter as shown in Block Assembly Diagram 2. Sew a background triangle to each diamond point. Sew 2 diamond sections together. Inset a background square to the joined diamond sections to complete a quarter. Repeat for the other 3 quarters. Sew the quarters together in pairs and then sew the 2 halves together. Add the shorter top and bottom borders, then add the longer side borders.
Make 4 blocks.

MAKING THE QUILT
Lay out the large Big Central Star points, background triangles and Small Corner Star blocks as shown in the Quilt Assembly Diagram. Arrange the large half-square triangles for the Central Big Star backgrounds so they are in pairs that will allow the print pattern to connect in the best possible way: with the wavy shapes running outwards from the centre of the star. (Use the photo of the quilt to see how this works.)

Using a ¼in (6mm) seam allowance, sew the large Central Big Star points, background triangles and Small Corner

49

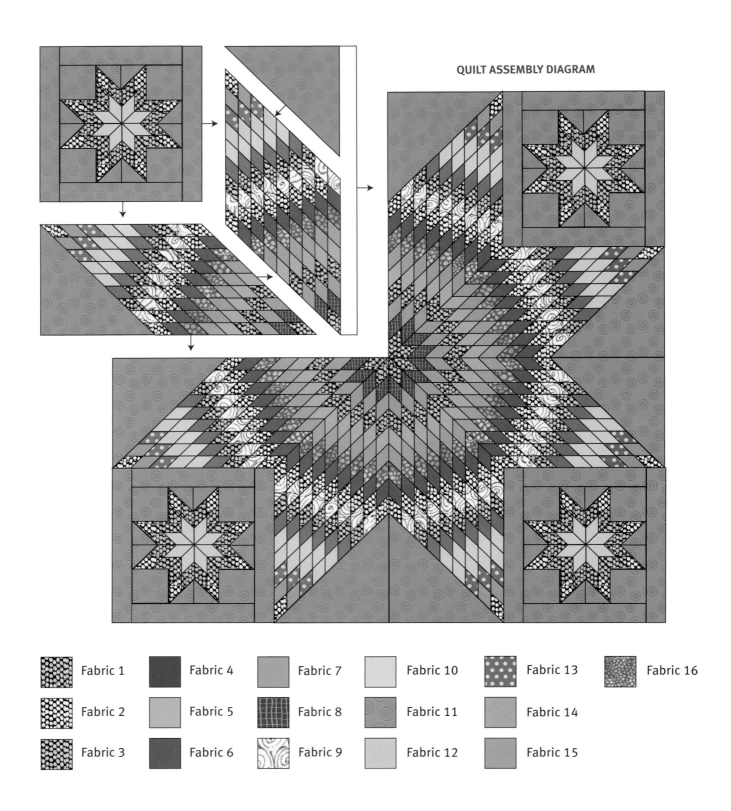

Fabric 1

Fabric 2

Fabric 3

Fabric 4

Fabric 5

Fabric 6

Fabric 7

Fabric 8

Fabric 9

Fabric 10

Fabric 11

Fabric 12

Fabric 13

Fabric 14

Fabric 15

Fabric 16

Star blocks together, quarter by quarter in the same way as the Small Corner Star blocks. Take care to match the diamond points and seams as you sew. Sew a large background triangle to each diamond point. Sew 2 diamond sections together. Inset a completed Small Corner Star block to the joined diamond sections to complete a quarter. Repeat for the other 3 quarters. Sew the quarters together in pairs and lastly, sew the two halves of the quilt top together.

FINISHING THE QUILT
Press the quilt top. Remove selvedges from the 3 backing fabric panels, pin and sew together using a ¼in (6mm) seam allowance. Trim one side to form a piece approx. 106in x 106 (270cm x 270cm). Layer the quilt top, batting and backing, and baste together (see page 140). Quilt as desired. Trim the quilt edges and attach the binding (see page 141).

midnight diamonds **

Kaffe Fassett

I dreamed up this layout for a previous book to show how easy it is to use large-scale prints. My new dark version has an exciting velvety depth. As it is a scrappy quilt, feel free to give it your own twist by using more of your favourite fabrics.

SIZE OF FINISHED QUILT
58in x 83.5in (147cm x 212cm)

FABRICS
Fabrics have been calculated at a maximum width of 40in (102cm. Fabrics have been given a number – see Fabric Swatch Diagram for details.

Patchwork Fabrics
Fabrics for diamonds in medium–large prints:

CACTUS FLOWER
Fabric 1	Black	½yd (45cm)
Fabric 2	Blue	½yd (45cm)

VARIEGATED MORNING GLORY
Fabric 3	Blue	½yd (45cm)

GEODES
Fabric 4	Black	½yd (45cm)

SEA URCHINS
Fabric 5	Antique	½yd (45cm)
Fabric 6	Red	½yd (45cm)

ROSE AND HYDRANGEA
Fabric 7	Blue	½yd (45cm)
Fabric 8	Navy	½yd (45cm)

TURKISH DELIGHT
Fabric 9	Wine	½yd (45cm)
Fabric 10	Black	½yd (45cm)

ROW FLOWERS
Fabric 11	Dark	½yd (45cm)

Fabrics for diamond borders in small–medium prints:

SPOT
Fabric 12	Plum	¼yd (25cm)
Fabric 13	Bottle	¼yd (25cm)
Fabric 14	Sapphire	¼yd (25cm)
Fabric 15	Peacock	¼yd (25cm)
Fabric 16	Forest	¼yd (25cm)

PAPER FANS
Fabric 17	Purple	¼yd (25cm)

GUINEA FLOWER
Fabric 18	Brown	¼yd (25cm)

BANG
Fabric 19	Blue	¼yd (25cm)

MAD PLAID
Fabric 20	Cobalt	¼yd (25cm)

CHIPS
Fabric 21	Charcoal	½ yd (45cm)

ONION RINGS
Fabric 22	Tomato	¼yd (25cm)

JUMBLE
Fabric 23	Ocean	¼yd (25cm)
Fabric 24	Blue	¼yd (25cm)
Fabric 25	Rust	¼yd (25cm)
Fabric 26	Ochre	¼yd (25cm)

ROMAN GLASS
Fabric 27	Purple	½yd (45cm)

Backing and Binding Fabrics
LOTUS LEAF
Fabric 28	Purple	5¼yd (4.8m)

ROMAN GLASS
Fabric 27	Purple	⅝yd (60cm)

Batting
66in x 92in (168cm x 234cm)

Clearview Triangle
A 60° acrylic ruler (optional)

TEMPLATES

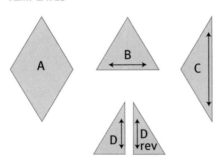

CUTTING OUT
Whole Diamonds
You will need 50 whole diamonds. Cut between 3 and 6 whole diamonds from each fabric using Template A. (Cut more from favourite fabrics and fewer from others.) Fussy cut some whole diamonds from the larger prints so there is an attractive display of the motifs in each patch. There is no need to position a single motif in the exact centre of the diamond – in fact the quilt will be livelier if the flowers and leaves are slightly off-centre.

Partial Diamonds
Do not fussy cut the partial diamonds (Templates B, C and D) for the sides, top, bottom and corners.
Cut Template B, C and D patches so the edge facing the outside edge of the quilt runs along the fabric grain as indicated on the template.
Cut 10 short half-diamonds using Template B for the top and bottom.
Cut 8 long half-diamonds using Template C for the sides.
Cut 2 quarter-diamonds using Template D and 2 using Template D reverse for the corners.

Diamond Borders
Each diamond border fabric will border 3–4 whole diamonds.
From each fabric cut 5 strips 1½in (3.8cm) wide across the fabric from selvedge to selvedge.
From the first 4 strips cut from each 1 length at 12in (30.5cm) and 2 lengths at 11in (28cm).
From the 5th strip cut 4 lengths at 9in (23cm).
Note: For fun, Kaffe used scraps of Fabric 4 as a border as well as diamonds.

Quilt Border
From Fabric 27 cut 8 strips 2in (5.1cm) wide from selvedge to selvedge. Remove the selvedges and sew end to end.

Backing
Remove selvedges and cut Fabric 28 in half across the width to make two pieces 94½in (240cm) long.

Binding
From the remaining Fabric 27 cut 8 strips 2½in (6.4cm) wide from selvedge to selvedge. Sew together end to end (see page 141).

FABRIC SWATCH DIAGRAM

Patchwork Fabrics

Fabric 1
CACTUS FLOWER
Black
PJ96BK

Fabric 2
CACTUS FLOWER
Blue
PJ96BL

Fabric 3
VARIEGATED MORNING GLORY
Blue
PJ98BL

Fabric 4
GEODES
Black
PJ99BK

Fabric 5
SEA URCHINS
Antique
PJ100AN

Fabric 6
SEA URCHINS
Red
PJ100RD

Fabric 7
ROSE AND HYDRANGEA
Blue
PJ97BL

Fabric 8
ROSE AND HYDRANGEA
Navy
PJ97NV

Fabric 9
TURKISH DELIGHT
Wine
GP81WN

Fabric 10
TURKISH DELIGHT
Black
GP81BK

Fabric 11
ROW FLOWERS
Dark
GP169DK

Fabric 12
SPOT
Plum
GP70PL

Fabric 13
SPOT
Bottle
GP70BT

Fabric 14
SPOT
Sapphire
GP70SP

Fabric 15
SPOT
Peacock
GP70PC

Fabric 16
SPOT
Forest
GP70FO

Fabric 17
PAPER FANS
Purple
GP143PU

Fabric 18
GUINEA FLOWER
Brown
GP59BR

Fabric 19
BANG
Blue
BM72BL

Fabric 20
MAD PLAID
Cobalt
BM37CB

Fabric 21
CHIPS
Charcoal
BM73CC

Fabric 22
ONION RINGS
Tomato
BM70TM

Fabric 23
JUMBLE
Ocean
BM53ON

Fabric 24
JUMBLE
Blue
BM53BL

Fabric 25
JUMBLE
Rust
BM53RU

Fabric 26
JUMBLE
Ochre
BM53OC

Fabric 27
ROMAN GLASS
Purple
GP01PU

Backing and Binding Fabrics

Fabric 28
LOTUS LEAF
Purple
GP29PU

Fabric 27
ROMAN GLASS
Purple
GP01PU

WHOLE DIAMOND BLOCK ASSEMBLY DIAGRAM

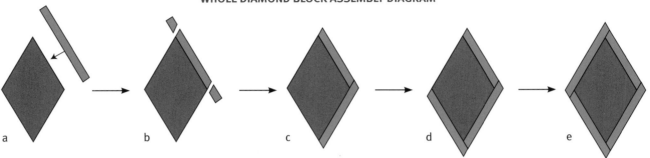

a   b   c   d   e

PARTIAL DIAMOND BLOCK ASSEMBLY DIAGRAMS

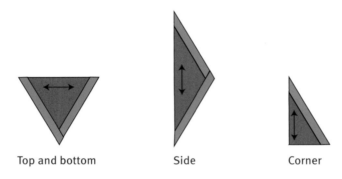

Top and bottom   Side   Corner

MAKING THE BLOCKS
Use a ¼in (6mm) seam allowance unless otherwise instructed.

Whole Diamonds
Choose a border fabric that contrasts well for each diamond patch. Follow the Whole Diamond Block Assembly Diagram to sew a border to each diamond, as follows: Sew a 9in (23cm) strip to the edge of the upper right side of the diamond (a). Press and trim off the ends of the strip so it aligns with the diamond (b). Sew an 11in (28cm) strip to the bottom right side in the same way, press and trim (c). Sew an 11in (28cm) strip to the bottom left side, press and trim (d). Sew a 12in (30.5cm) strip to the top left side, press and trim (e).

Partial Diamonds
Referring to the Partial Diamond Block Assembly Diagrams, make 10 top and bottom partial diamond blocks with straight grain on the open side. Make 8 side partial diamond blocks, leaving the long edge open, not bordered, with an 11in (28cm) strip and a 12in (30.5cm)

strip for each. Make 4 corner partial diamond blocks with a border only on the diagonal side, using a 12in (30.5cm) strip for each.

MAKING THE QUILT
Arrange the blocks and partial blocks in 9 alternating rows of 6 and 5 patches using the photograph and Quilt Assembly Diagram as a guide. Fabric numbers for the diamonds have been included on the diagram should you wish to copy the layout exactly. Begin by laying out the 50 whole diamonds then add partial diamonds to complete the layout. Use a ¼in (6mm) seam allowance throughout and refer to the Quilt Assembly Diagram for assembly. Sew the diamonds together in diagonal rows, press seams then sew the diagonal rows together, carefully matching seam junctions and points as you sew.

Quilt Borders
Note: Approximate measurements for the side borders will be 80½in (204.5cm) and for the top and bottom borders

58in (147.3cm), but check your quilt measurements before cutting as sizes can vary depending on cutting, sewing machines and sewing styles.
Measure the main body of the quilt end to end through the centre and cut 2 pieces of border Fabric 27 to this measurement. Pin, sew on side borders and press. Measure the quilt (including side borders) from side to side across the centre and cut 2 pieces of border Fabric 27 to this measurement. Pin, sew to the top and bottom and press.

FINISHING THE QUILT
Press the quilt top. Sew the 2 pieces of backing Fabric 28 together along the long side. Trim to approximately 66in (168cm) wide x 92in (234cm) long.
Layer the quilt top, batting and backing, and baste together (see page 140).
Quilt as desired.
Trim the quilt edges and attach the binding (see page 141).

Fabric 1, 2, 3, 4, 5, 6, 7, 8, 9, 10, 11

Fabric 12, 13, 14, 15, 16, 17, 18, 19, 20, 21, 22, 23, 24, 25, 26

Fabric 27

tawny pinwheels **

Kaffe Fassett

Setting the pinwheels on point gives them an elegant difference from the square-on versions. Brandon's Bali Brocade, cut across the wavy stripe, makes a jaunty border. The quilt has two traditional blocks: a feature fabric square-in-a-square block and a pinwheel block. The blocks are arranged on point in alternating rows, creating a further block pattern.

SIZE OF FINISHED QUILT
84½in x 101½in (215cm x 258cm)

FABRICS
Fabrics have been calculated at a maximum width of 40in (102cm), and are cut across the width, unless otherwise stated. Fabrics have been given a number – see Fabric Swatch Diagram for details.

Patchwork Fabrics
MAD PLAID
Fabric 1   Maroon   1⅝yd (1.5m)
* see also Binding Fabric
BALI BROCADE
Fabric 2   Ochre   3¼yd (2.9m)
JUMBLE
Fabric 3   Tangerine   ½yd (45cm)
SHARK'S TEETH
Fabric 4   Orange   ½yd (45cm)
GOOD VIBRATIONS
Fabric 5   Purple   ½yd (45cm)
ZIG ZAG
Fabric 6   Gold   ½yd (45cm)
ROMAN GLASS
Fabric 7   Gold   ½yd (45cm)
MILLEFIORE
Fabric 8   Orange   ½yd (45cm)
SPOT
Fabric 9   Royal   ½yd (45cm)
Fabric 10   Orange   ½yd (45cm)
GUINEA FLOWER
Fabric 11   Brown   ⅝yd (60cm)
KYOTO
Fabric 12   Orange   ⅜yd (40cm)
TURKISH DELIGHT
Fabric 13   Gold   ⅜yd (40cm)
CACTUS FLOWER
Fabric 14   Yellow   ⅜yd (40cm)
ROSE AND HYDRANGEA
Fabric 15   Citrus   ⅜yd (40cm)
VARIEGATED MORNING GLORY
Fabric 16   Orange   ⅜yd (40cm)

FABRIC SWATCH DIAGRAM

Patchwork Fabrics

Fabric 1
MAD PLAID
Maroon
BM37MR

Fabric 2
BALI BROCADE
Ochre
BM69OC

Fabric 3
JUMBLE
Tangerine
BM53TN

Fabric 4
SHARK'S TEETH
Orange
BM60OR

Fabric 5
GOOD VIBRATIONS
Purple
BM65PU

Fabric 6
ZIG ZAG
Gold
BM43GD

Fabric 7
ROMAN GLASS
Gold
GP01GD

Fabric 8
MILLEFIORE
Orange
GP92OR

Fabric 9
SPOT
Royal
GP70RY

Fabric 10
SPOT
Orange
GP70OR

Fabric 11
GUINEA FLOWER
Brown
GP59BR

Fabric 12
KYOTO
Orange
KF08OR

Fabric 13
TURKISH DELIGHT
Gold
GP81GD

Fabric 14
CACTUS FLOWER
Yellow
PJ96YE

Fabric 15
ROSE AND HYDRANGEA
Citrus
PJ97CT

Fabric 16
VARIEGATED MORNING GLORY
Orange
PJ98OR

Backing and Binding Fabrics

Fabric 17
BRASSICA
Orange
PJ51OR

Fabric 1
MAD PLAID
Maroon
BM37MR

Backing and Binding Fabrics
BRASSICA
Fabric 17   Orange   8yd (7.4m)
MAD PLAID
Fabric 1   Maroon   ¾yd (70cm)
* see also Patchwork Fabrics

Batting
93in x 110in (236cm x 279cm)

CUTTING OUT
All patches are cut from strips cut across the width of the fabric.

Square-in-a-square Blocks
The following shapes are cut from 9in (23cm) strips: 12 large squares 9in x 9in (23cm x 23cm); 14 half-squares (rectangles) 4¾in x 9in (12.1cm x 23cm); and 4 quarter-squares (small squares) 4¾in x 4¾in (12.1cm x 12.1cm). Cut as instructed from the following:
Fabric 2 2 large squares;
Fabric 12 3 large squares and 2 half-squares;
Fabric 13 2 large squares, 2 half-squares and 2 quarter-squares;
Fabric 14 1 large square, 3 half-squares and 1 quarter-square;
Fabric 15 2 large squares, 3 half-squares and 1 quarter-square;
Fabric 16 2 large squares and 4 half-squares.

Surrounding Triangles
From Fabric 1 cut triangles for surrounding the large squares as follows: From 4 strips 9¾in (24.8cm) wide, cross cut 16 squares 9¾in x 9¾in (24.8cm x 24.8cm). Cut each square diagonally twice to make 4 triangles from each square (you will have 2 extra triangles). From 3 strips 5⅛in (13.1cm) wide, cross cut 18 squares at 5⅛in x 5⅛in (13.1cm x 13.1cm). Cut each square diagonally once to make 2 triangles from each, 36 in total.

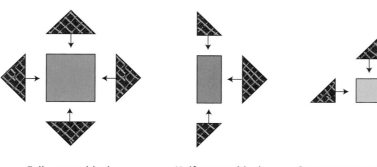

Full-square block   Half-square block   Quarter-square block

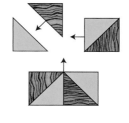

Pinwheel Blocks

Cut strips $6^{7}/_{8}$in (17.5cm) wide across the width of the fabric and cross cut squares $6^{7}/_{8}$in x $6^{7}/_{8}$in (17.5cm x 17.5cm). Cut each square diagonally once to make 2 triangles from each, 160 triangles in total. Cut squares from fabrics as follows:

Fabric 3 – light (2 strips) 6 squares, 12 triangles;

Fabric 4 – dark (2 strips) 10 squares, 20 triangles;

Fabric 5 – dark (2 strips) 10 squares, 20 triangles;

Fabric 6 – light (2 strips) 8 squares, 16 triangles;

Fabric 7 – light (2 strips) 10 squares, 20 triangles;

Fabric 8 – light (2 strips) 10 squares, 20 triangles;

Fabric 9 – light (2 strips) 8 squares, 16 triangles;

Fabric 10 – light (2 strips) 6 squares, 12 triangles;

Fabric 11 – light (2 strips) 12 squares, 24 triangles.

Border

Note: Fabric 2 Bali Brocade is very large scale. Strips are cut from selvedge to selvedge and then the pattern is matched as closely as possible to get the lengths needed for each border. Seams will not match exactly, but as the overall pattern is wavy there will be a 'bulge' that goes in one direction when cut. When sewing border strips end to end, make sure the 'bulge' goes in the same direction; seam the fabric at a spot that comes close to matching the pattern (about 6in/15.2cm will be wasted at the end of each strip). From Fabric 2 cut 12 strips $8^{1}/_{2}$in (21.6cm)

wide. Remove selvedges and sew end to end as described above. From the total length cut 2 pieces $85^{1}/_{2}$in (217cm) for the sides and 2 pieces $84^{1}/_{2}$in (214.6cm) for the top and bottom.

Note: Mark which is which.

Backing

From Fabric 17 cut 3 lengths approximately $92^{1}/_{2}$in (235cm) long.

Binding

From Fabric 1 cut 10 strips $2^{1}/_{2}$in (6.4cm) wide and sew end to end (see page 141).

MAKING THE BLOCKS

Square-in-a-square Blocks

Follow Block Assembly Diagram 1 to make the blocks from Fabric 1 surrounding triangles and the large floral squares, half-squares and quarter-squares. For each square or part-square, first sew opposite triangles to the centre square/part-square, press, then sew on the remaining triangle(s). Complete 12 full-square blocks, 14 half-square blocks and 4 quarter-square blocks.

Pinwheel Blocks

Follow Block Assembly Diagram 2 to make 20 Pinwheel blocks each from 4 dark triangles and 4 light triangles. Use the quilt photograph and the Quilt Assembly Diagram as a guide and match the fabrics, or select your own combinations of light and dark triangles for each block. (Shades marked in the Cutting Out section). Sew 4 matching pairs of light and dark triangles together, press and sew squares together in pairs and then sew 2 pairs of squares together,

ensuring points are positioned correctly to form the Pinwheel pattern.

MAKING THE QUILT

The blocks are arranged on point so the rows will be diagonal. Using a $^{1}/_{4}$in (6mm) seam allowance throughout, follow the photograph for block placement and sew the blocks together into diagonal rows as shown in the Quilt Assembly Diagram (see page 60). Press and sew the rows together.

Borders

Keeping the 'bulge' pattern in Fabric 2 Bali Brocade going in one direction so that it travels around the quilt as in the photograph (refer to Cutting Out: Border), sew the 2 longer $85^{1}/_{2}$in (217cm) border pieces to the sides and press. Sew the 2 shorter $84^{1}/_{2}$in (215cm) border pieces to the top and bottom.

FINISHING THE QUILT

Press the quilt top. Sew the 3 backing pieces together using a $^{1}/_{4}$in (6mm) seam allowance to form a piece approximately 93in x 120in (236cm x 305cm). Trim to approximately 93in x 110in (236cm x 279cm).

Layer the quilt top, batting and backing, and baste together (see page 140).

Quilt as desired.

Trim the quilt edges and attach the binding (see page 141).

QUILT ASSEMBLY DIAGRAM

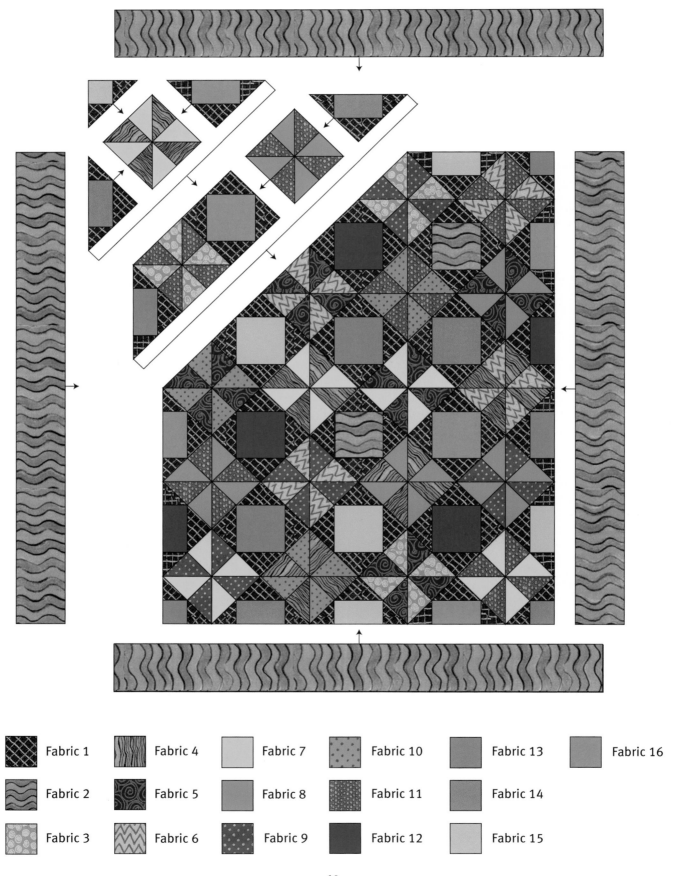

Fabric 1
Fabric 2
Fabric 3
Fabric 4
Fabric 5
Fabric 6
Fabric 7
Fabric 8
Fabric 9
Fabric 10
Fabric 11
Fabric 12
Fabric 13
Fabric 14
Fabric 15
Fabric 16

smouldering stars **

Kaffe Fassett

This is another tonal story, here with smouldering tones of embers with shots of rich cobalt and emerald to cool it a little. A slightly larger quilt than *Sunshine Stars* from *Kaffe Quilts Again*, it also uses the very traditional, geometric Ohio Star block.

SIZE OF FINISHED QUILT
72½in x 84½in (184cm x 215cm)

FABRICS
Fabrics have been calculated at a maximum width of 40in (102cm), and are cut across the width, unless otherwise stated. Fabrics have been given a number – see Fabric Swatch Diagram for details.

Patchwork Fabrics
GEODES
| Fabric 1 | Black | ¼yd (25cm) |
| Fabric 2 | Red | ¼yd (25cm) |

PAPER FANS
Fabric 3	Red	¼yd (25cm)
Fabric 4	Black	½yd (45cm)
Fabric 5	Purple	¼yd (25cm)

ONION RINGS
| Fabric 6 | Cocoa | ½yd (45cm) |
| Fabric 7 | Tomato | ¼yd (25cm) |

CHIPS
| Fabric 8 | Charcoal | ¼yd (25cm) |
| Fabric 9 | Purple | ¼yd (25cm) |

JUMBLE
| Fabric 10 | Orange | ½yd (45cm) |
* see also Binding Fabric

PRIMULAS
| Fabric 11 | Blue | ½yd (45cm) |

GUINEA FLOWER
| Fabric 12 | Red | ½yd (45cm) |

SPOT
| Fabric 13 | Forest | ½yd (45cm) |
| Fabric 14 | Violet | ⅝yd (60cm) |

SHOT COTTON
Fabric 15	Prune	½yd (45cm)
Fabric 16	Thunder	¼yd (25cm)
Fabric 17	Steel	½yd (45cm)

WOVEN MULTI STRIPE
| Fabric 18 | Pimento | ½yd (45cm) |

SHARK'S TEETH
| Fabric 19 | Orange | ¼yd (25cm) |

ROMAN GLASS
| Fabric 20 | Purple | ¼yd (25cm) |

SEA URCHINS
| Fabric 21 | Red | ½yd (45cm) |

BANG
| Fabric 22 | Red | ¼yd (25cm) |

Border Fabric
TURKISH DELIGHT
| Fabric 23 | Wine | 2⅛yd (2m) |

Backing and Binding Fabrics
FRUIT MANDALA
Extra Wide Backing
| Fabric 24 | Pink | 2¼yd (2.1m) |
JUMBLE
| Fabric 10 | Orange | ¾yd (70cm) |
* see also Patchwork Fabrics

Batting
81 x 93in (206cm x 236cm)

PATCH SHAPES
Two square patch shapes (Square A and Square B) and 2 triangle patch shapes (Triangle C and Triangle D) are pieced together to make traditional Ohio Star blocks.

CUTTING OUT
All patches are cut from strips across the width of the fabric, then cross cut into squares and triangles as described. Refer to the Cutting Diagram and Cutting Table. Cut the patches in the order specified, always keeping remaining fabric in the largest piece possible. Remove all selvages before cutting out.

Triangle C (Background Inset Triangle)
Cut a strip 7¼in (18.4cm) wide and cut squares at 7¼in (18.4cm). Cut each square diagonally twice to make 4 triangles from each square. Cut required pieces from fabrics as shown in the Cutting Table.

Square B (Background Corners)
Trim the remainder of each strip of fabric to 7in (17.8cm) wide and cut 3½in (8.9cm) rectangles. Cross cut each rectangle into 2 squares 3½in (8.9cm). Cut required pieces from fabrics as shown in the Cutting Table.

Square A (Star Centre)
Trim the remainder of each strip of fabric to 6½in (16.5cm) wide, or cut a strip 6½in (16.5cm) wide if required and cut 6½in (16.5cm) squares. Cut required pieces from fabrics as shown in the Cutting Table.

Triangle D (Star Points)
Trim the remainder of each strip of fabric to 3⅞in (9.8cm) strips, or cut a strip 3⅞in (9.8cm) wide if required, and cut 3⅞in (9.8cm) squares. Cut each square once diagonally to make 2 triangles from each square. Cut required pieces from fabrics as shown in the Cutting Table.

CUTTING DIAGRAM

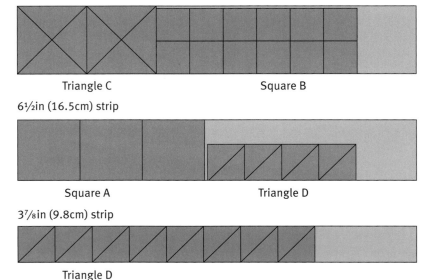

7¼in (18.4cm) strip

Triangle C   Square B

6½in (16.5cm) strip

Square A   Triangle D

3⅞in (9.8cm) strip

Triangle D

FABRIC SWATCH DIAGRAM

Patchwork Fabrics

Fabric 1
GEODES
Black
PJ99BK

Fabric 2
GEODES
Red
PJ99RD

Fabric 3
PAPER FANS
Red
GP143RD

Fabric 4
PAPER FANS
Black
GP143BK

Fabric 5
PAPER FANS
Purple
GP143PU

Fabric 6
ONION RINGS
Cocoa
BM70CO

Fabric 7
ONION RINGS
Tomato
BM70TM

Fabric 8
CHIPS
Charcoal
BM73CC

Fabric 9
CHIPS
Purple
BM73PU

Fabric 10
JUMBLE
Orange
BM53OR

Fabric 11
PRIMULAS
Blue
BM71BL

Fabric 12
GUINEA FLOWER
Red
GP59RD

Fabric 13
SPOT
Forest
GP70FO

Fabric 14
SPOT
Violet
GP70VI

Fabric 15
SHOT COTTON
Prune
SC03PR

Fabric 16
SHOT COTTON
Thunder
SC06TH

Fabric 17
SHOT COTTON
Steel
SC75ST

Fabric 18
WOVEN MULTI STRIPE
Pimento
WMUL01PI

Fabric 19
SHARK'S TEETH
Orange
BM60OR

Fabric 20
ROMAN GLASS
Purple
GP01PU

Fabric 21
SEA URCHINS
Red
PJ100RD

Fabric 22
BANG
Red
BM72RD

Fabric 23
TURKISH DELIGHT
Wine
GP81WN

Backing and Binding Fabrics

Fabric 24
FRUIT MANDALA
Pink
QB03PK

Fabric 10
JUMBLE
Orange
BM53OR

CUTTING TABLE

Patch:	Triangle C	Square B	Square A	Triangle D
	4 per square	2 per rectangle	1 square	2 per square
SQUARES	7¼in (18.4cm)	3½in (8.9cm)	6½in (16.5cm)	3⅞in (9.8cm)
Fabric 1	1	4	1	4
Fabric 2	1	4	1	4
Fabric 3	1	4	1	4
Fabric 4	2	8	2	8
Fabric 5	1	4	1	4
Fabric 6	2	8	2	8
Fabric 7	1	4	1	4
Fabric 8	1	4	1	4
Fabric 9	1	4	1	4
Fabric 10	1	4	2	8
Fabric 11	2	8	2	8
Fabric 12	2	8	1	4
Fabric 13	2	8	1	4
Fabric 14	2	8	3	12
Fabric 15	2	8	1	4
Fabric 16	1	4	1	4
Fabric 17	1	4	2	8
Fabric 18	2	8	1	4
Fabric 19	1	4	1	4
Fabric 20	1	4	1	4
Fabric 21	1	4	2	8
Fabric 22	1	4	1	4
Total squares	30	120	30	120
TRIANGLES	120 QST			240 HST

Borders

From Fabric 23 fussy cut 4 strips 6½in x 72½in (16.5cm x 184cm) down the length of the fabric, parallel to the selvedge, positioning large motifs centrally along each strip.

Backing

From Fabric 24 cut one piece 81in x 93in (206cm x 236cm).

Binding

From Fabric 10 cut 9 Strips 2½in (6.4cm) wide. Sew end to end (see page 141).

MAKING THE QUILT

Using a ¼in (6mm) seam allowance throughout, piece 30 blocks as shown in the Block Assembly Diagram. Refer to the Quilt Assembly Diagram for fabric placement. Sew the blocks into 6 rows of 5 blocks, then sew the rows together to make the quilt centre.

ADDING THE BORDERS

Referring to the Quilt Assembly Diagram, sew a 6½in x 72½in (16.5cm x 184cm) border to each side of the quilt centre. Press then sew the remaining 6½in x 72½in (16.5cm x 184cm) borders to the top and bottom to complete the quilt.

FINISHING THE QUILT

Press the quilt top and backing. Layer the quilt top, batting and backing, and baste together (see page 140).
Quilt as desired.
Trim the quilt edges and attach the binding (see page 141).

BLOCK ASSEMBLY DIAGRAM

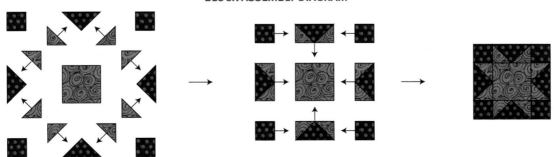

QUILT ASSEMBLY DIAGRAM

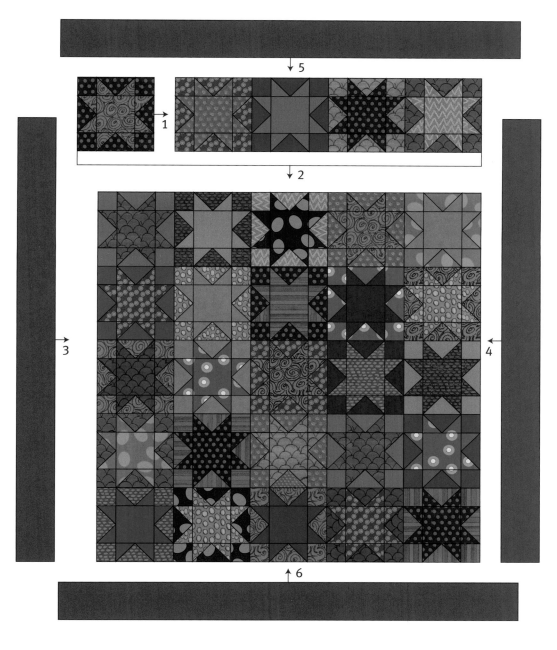

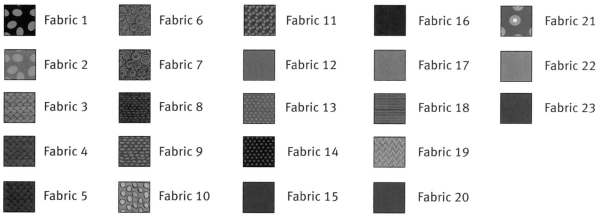

Fabric 1   Fabric 6   Fabric 11   Fabric 16   Fabric 21

Fabric 2   Fabric 7   Fabric 12   Fabric 17   Fabric 22

Fabric 3   Fabric 8   Fabric 13   Fabric 18   Fabric 23

Fabric 4   Fabric 9   Fabric 14   Fabric 19

Fabric 5   Fabric 10   Fabric 15   Fabric 20

ocean ripples *

Kaffe Fassett

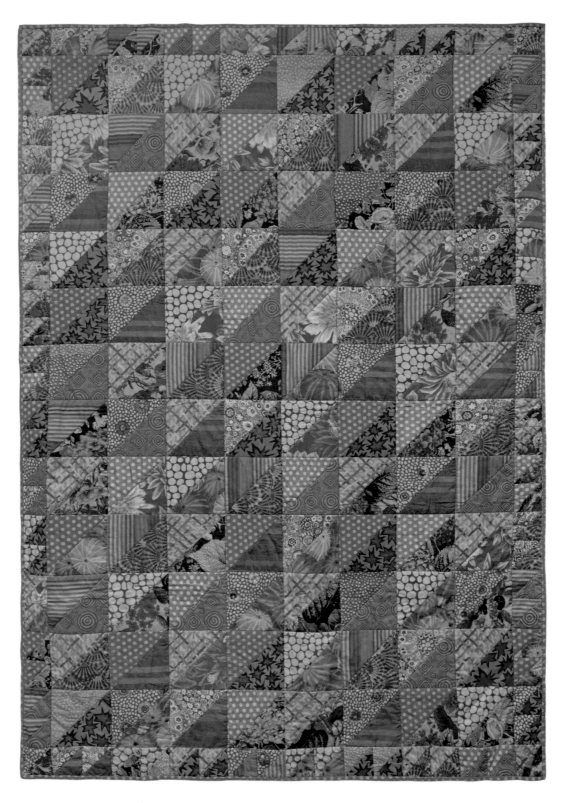

Keeping this palette to cool shades of blue and green makes me dream of the gorgeous tones of the sea. I'm so grateful we have so many shades to combine here. This modest combination of half-square triangles in darker and lighter tones is simple but very effective.

FABRIC SWATCH DIAGRAM

Patchwork Fabrics

Fabric 1
ROSE AND HYDRANGEA
Navy
PJ97NV

Fabric 2
ROSE AND HYDRANGEA
Blue
PJ97BL

Fabric 3
SPOT
Sapphire
GP70SP

Fabric 4
SPOT
Guava
GP70GU

Fabric 5
MILLEFIORE
Aqua
GP92AQ

Fabric 6
OMBRE
Red
GP117RD

Fabric 7
SEA URCHINS
Blue
PJ100BL

Fabric 8
PAPER FANS
Purple
GP143PU

Fabric 9
GOOD VIBRATIONS
Teal
BM65TE

Fabric 10
BANG
Blue
BM72BL

Fabric 11
BROAD STRIPE
Blue
WBROBL

Fabric 12
CATERPILLAR STRIPE
Blue
WCATBL

Fabric 13
CACTUS FLOWER
Blue
PJ96BL

Fabric 14
GUINEA FLOWER
Cobalt
GP59CB

Fabric 15
MAD PLAID
Turquoise
BM37TQ

Fabric 16
JUMBLE
Duck Egg
BM53DE

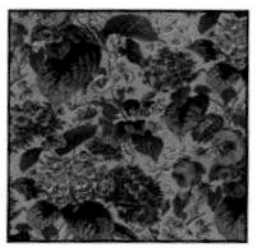

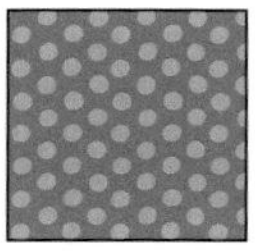

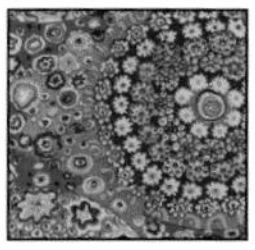

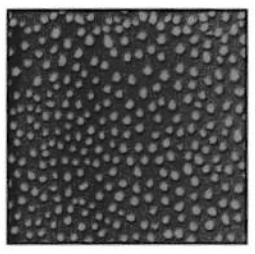

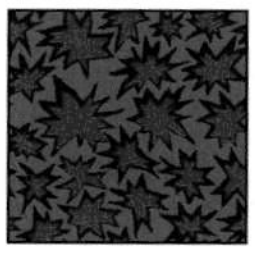

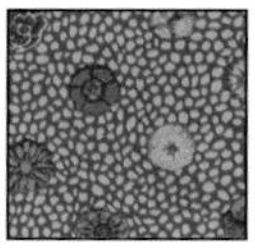

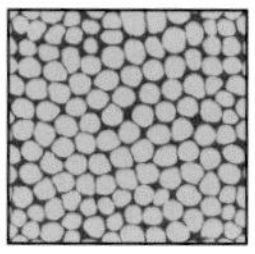

Backing and Binding Fabrics

Fabric 17
MOSS
Blue
BM68BL

Fabric 3
SPOT
Sapphire
GP70SP

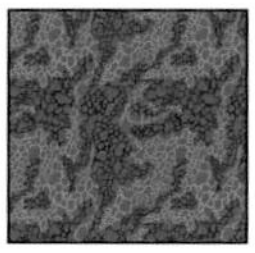

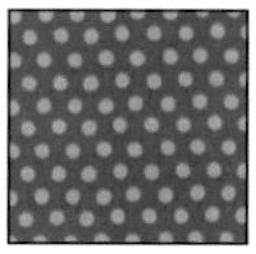

SIZE OF FINISHED QUILT
54.5in x 78.5in (138cm x 199cm)

FABRICS
Fabrics have been calculated at a maximum width of 40in (102cm), and are cut across the width, unless otherwise stated. Fabrics have been given a number – see Fabric Swatch Diagram for details.

Patchwork Fabrics
ROSE AND HYDRANGEA

Fabric 1	Navy	½yd (45cm)
Fabric 2	Blue	½yd (45cm)

SPOT

Fabric 3	Sapphire	½yd (45cm)

* see also Binding Fabric

Fabric 4	Guava	½yd (45cm)

MILLEFIORE

Fabric 5	Aqua	½yd (45cm)

OMBRE

Fabric 6	Red	¼yd (25cm)

SEA URCHINS

Fabric 7	Blue	⅝yd (60cm)

PAPER FANS

Fabric 8	Purple	½yd (45cm)

GOOD VIBRATIONS

Fabric 9	Teal	½yd (45cm)

BANG

Fabric 10	Blue	⅝yd (60cm)

BROAD STRIPE

Fabric 11	Blue	½yd (45cm)

CATERPILLAR STRIPE

Fabric 12	Blue	½yd (45cm)

CACTUS FLOWER

Fabric 13	Blue	⅜yd (40cm)

GUINEA FLOWER

Fabric 14	Cobalt	½yd (45cm)

MAD PLAID

Fabric 15	Turquoise	⅝yd (60cm)

JUMBLE

Fabric 16	Duck Egg	½yd (45cm)

Backing and Binding Fabrics
MOSS

Fabric 17	Blue	5yd (4.5m)

SPOT

Fabric 3	Sapphire	⅝yd (60cm)

* see also Patchwork Fabrics

Batting
63in x 87in (160cm x 221cm)

PATCH SHAPES

All patches are square, cut from strips, cross cut diagonally and sewn in pairs to form half-square triangle (HST) blocks. The main body of the quilt is formed of large HST blocks measuring 6in (15.2cm) finished. The border is formed of small HST blocks measuring 3in (7.6cm) finished.

CUTTING OUT

Following are cutting instructions to create an exact copy of the original quilt. Alternatively, as this is essentially a scrappy quilt, you could choose fabrics in 8 medium and 8 dark tones, and place triangles randomly in light and dark pairs. This is a great way to personalize the design, and you can use more or less of certain fabrics as you choose. Also bear in mind there is ample fabric to vary the number of triangles you cut from each. Cut strips from the width of the fabric and then cross cut as described.

Large Half-square Triangles (HSTs)
Cut strips 6⅞in (17.5cm) wide and cross cut squares 6⅞in (17.5cm). Each strip will give you 5 squares. Cut each square once diagonally to make 2 HST triangles from each square. Cut from the following:
Fabric 1 (2 strips) 6 squares, 12 triangles;
Fabric 2 (2 strips) 6 squares, 12 triangles;
Fabric 3 (2 strips) 7 squares, 13 triangles;
Fabric 4 (2 strips) 6 squares, 12 triangles;
Fabric 5 (2 strips) 6 squares, 12 triangles;
Fabric 6 (1 strip) 3 squares, 5 triangles;
Fabric 7 (2 strips) 7 squares, 13 triangles;
Fabric 8 (2 strips) 6 squares, 12 triangles;
Fabric 9 (2 strips) 6 squares, 12 triangles;
Fabric 10 (2 strips) 7 squares, 13 triangles;
Fabric 11 (2 strips) 6 squares, 12 triangles;
Fabric 12 (2 strips) 6 squares, 12 triangles;
Fabric 13 (1 strip) 5 squares, 10 triangles;
Fabric 14 (2 strips) 6 squares, 12 triangles;
Fabric 15 (2 strips) 9 squares, 18 triangles;
Fabric 16 (2 strips) 6 squares, 12 triangles.
Total of 192 triangles.

Small Half-square Triangles (Border)
From the surplus fabrics from the large HSTs, trim left-over strips down to, or cut new strips at, 3⅞in (9.8cm) wide and cross cut squares 3⅞in (9.8cm). Each full strip will give you 10 squares. Cut each square once diagonally to make 2 small HST triangles from each square. Cut from the following:

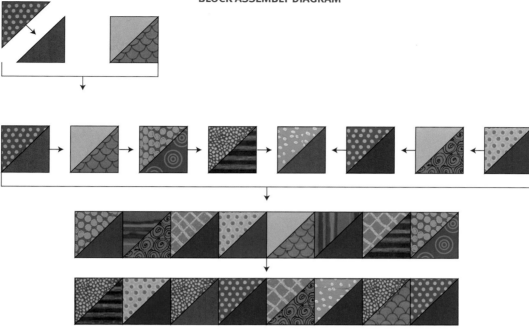

Fabric 1 5 squares, 10 triangles;
Fabric 2 6 squares, 11 triangles;
Fabric 3 3 squares, 6 triangles;
Fabric 4 5 squares, 10 triangles;
Fabric 5 7 squares, 13 triangles;
Fabric 6 3 squares, 6 triangles;
Fabric 7 (1 strip) 7 squares, 14 triangles;
Fabric 8 5 squares, 9 triangles;
Fabric 9 6 squares, 12 triangles;
Fabric 10 (1 strip) 7 squares, 14 triangles;
Fabric 11 2 squares, 4 triangles;
Fabric 12 8 squares, 16 triangles;
Fabric 13 (1 strip) 2 squares, 4 triangles;
Fabric 14 5 squares, 9 triangles;
Fabric 15 (1 strip) 10 squares,
20 triangles;
Fabric 16 5 squares, 10 triangles.
Total of 168 triangles.

Backing
From Fabric 17 cut 1 piece of fabric 40in x 87in (102cm x 221cm), and 1 piece 23in x 87in (58cm x 221cm). Remove selvedges and sew together to make a piece 63in x 87in (160cm x 221cm).

Binding
From Fabric 3 cut 8 strips 2½in (6.4cm) wide and sew end to end (see page 141).

MAKING THE QUILT
Centre Blocks
Use a ¼in (6mm) seam allowance throughout. Where possible press seams towards the dark fabric.

Quilt Centre Blocks
Use a design wall to help to place the patches in the correct design layout. Each large HST block follows a dark and light pattern to create a ripple effect. Referring to the photograph, the Block Assembly Diagram and the Quilt Assembly Diagram for fabric combinations, pair triangles (dark with light) and sew together along the long diagonal edge to make each large HST block. As these are bias seams, try not to pull the seam as you sew it. Total of 96 large HST blocks.
Following the Quilt Assembly Diagram, sew 12 horizontal rows of 8 large HST blocks to make the centre of the quilt.

Border Blocks
Following the same dark and light pattern as the large HST blocks in the quilt centre, and using the photograph and Quilt Assembly Diagram as a guide, sew a light and dark triangle together along

their long diagonal edges to make each small HST unit. Make 80 small HST blocks in pairs (so you have 2 HSTs blocks from the same fabrics). Also make 4 single blocks for the corners. Arrange the small HST blocks in matching pairs around the border with a single block in each corner.

Following the Quilt Assembly Diagram (see page 70) piece 2 strips of 12 pairs of small HST blocks for the side borders of the quilt. Piece 2 strips of 8 pairs of small HST blocks for the top and bottom borders of the quilt top, and add a single corner block at each end. Attach the side borders to the quilt top, carefully matching seams to the centre block seams. Attach the top and bottom borders including the corner units to the top and bottom of the quilt top, again matching seams to the centre block seams.

FINISHING THE QUILT
Layer the quilt top, batting and backing, and baste together (see page 140).
Quilt as desired.
Trim the quilt edges and attach the binding (see page 141).

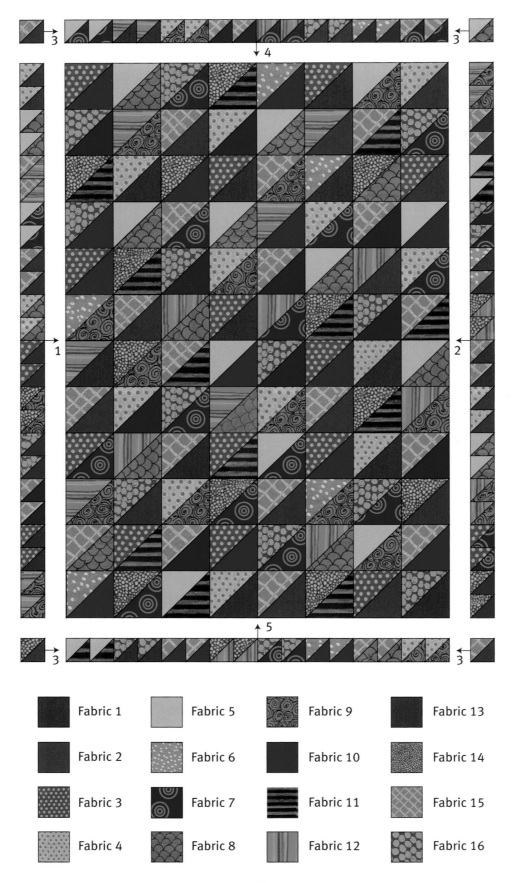

Fabric 1   Fabric 5   Fabric 9   Fabric 13

Fabric 2   Fabric 6   Fabric 10   Fabric 14

Fabric 3   Fabric 7   Fabric 11   Fabric 15

Fabric 4   Fabric 8   Fabric 12   Fabric 16

dark garden *

Kaffe Fassett

In this deep, rich quilt, the large Millefiore fabric triangles create dramatic shadows. The large print fabrics used for the small squares in each block create a lively contrast against the small prints of the triangles that edge them.

SIZE OF FINISHED QUILT
75½ in x 65½ in (192cm x 166cm)

FABRICS
Fabrics have been calculated at a maximum width of 40in (102cm), and are cut across the width, unless otherwise stated. Fabrics have been given a number – see Fabric Swatch Diagram for details.

Patchwork Fabrics
SHAGGY
Fabric 1   Black   ⅜yd (40cm)
LAKE BLOSSOMS
Fabric 2   Black   ⅜yd (40cm)
BIG BLOOMS
Fabric 3   Emerald   ¼yd (25cm)
CACTUS FLOWER
Fabric 4   Black   ¼yd (25cm)
Fabric 5   Red   ¼yd (25cm)
JUMBLE
Fabric 6   Purple   ⅜yd (40cm)
GOOD VIBRATIONS
Fabric 7   Teal   ⅜yd (40cm)
ROSE AND HYDRANGEA
Fabric 8   Blue   ⅜ yd (40cm)
Fabric 9   Navy   ¼yd (25cm)
MILLEFIORE
Fabric 10   Dark   2yd (1.9m)
ABORIGINAL DOT
Fabric 11   Plum   ⅜yd (40cm)
Fabric 12   Denim   ⅜yd (40cm)
Fabric 13   Orchid   ⅝yd (60cm)
SPOT
Fabric 14   Sapphire   ⅜yd (40cm)
Fabric 15   Forest   ⅜yd (40cm)
Fabric 16   Green   ⅜yd (40cm)
Fabric 17   Purple   ⅜yd (40cm)
Fabric 18   Peacock   ⅜yd (40cm)
Fabric 19   Royal   ⅜yd (40cm)
GUINEA FLOWER
Fabric 20   Brown   ⅜yd (40cm)
ONION RINGS
Fabric 21   Tomato   ⅜yd (40cm)

Backing and Binding Fabrics
FRUIT MANDALA
Fabric 22   Blue   2½yd (2.3m)
SPOT
Fabric 23   Black   ⅝yd (60cm)

Batting
84in x 74in (213cm x 188cm)

PATCHES
The mid-toned, large-scale square patches, fussy cut featuring a flower in each, are 5in (12.7cm) finished. The remaining patches (dark large triangles, mid-toned small triangles and border squares) are cut from strips.

CUTTING OUT
Cut the fabrics from the width of the fabric and then cross cut as described. Some of the fabrics are fussy cut.

Feature Squares
Fussy cut 5½in (14cm) squares, making sure a flower is featured. Cut 30 squares from mid-toned fabrics as follows:
Fabric 1   7 squares;
Fabric 2   4 squares;
Fabric 3   3 squares;
Fabric 4   4 squares;
Fabric 5   4 squares;
Fabric 8   6 squares;
Fabric 9   2 squares.

Large Triangles
From Fabric 10 cut 5 strips at 10⅞in (27.6cm) wide and cross cut 10⅞in (27.6cm) squares. Three squares can be cut from each strip. Cut each of the 15 squares diagonally once to make 2 triangles from each, making a total of 30 triangles. Remaining fabric will be used to make dark border squares.

Small Triangles
Cut strips 5⅞in (14.9cm) wide and cross cut squares 5⅞in (14.9cm). 6 squares can be cut from each strip. Cut each square diagonally once to make 2 triangles from each. Remaining fabric will be used to make the border squares. Cut squares as follows from:
Fabric 6   5 squares, 10 triangles;
Fabric 7   2 squares, 4 triangles;
Fabric 11 2 squares, 4 triangles;
Fabric 12 3 squares, 6 triangles;
Fabric 14 2 squares, 4 triangles;
Fabric 15 2 squares, 4 triangles;
Fabric 16 2 squares, 4 triangles;
Fabric 17 3 squares, 6 triangles;
Fabric 18 2 squares, 4 triangles;
Fabric 19 2 squares, 4 triangles;
Fabric 20 3 squares, 6 triangles;
Fabric 21 2 squares, 4 triangles.

Border Square Patches
Using the leftover fabrics, cut strips 3in (7.6cm) wide and cross cut 3in (7.6cm) squares. (13 squares can be cut from a full-width strip.)
Dark squares Cut as follows from:
Fabric 10 (4 strips plus remaining fabric from large triangles) 78 squares;
Fabric 13 (6 strips) 72 squares.
Total 150 dark squares.
Mid-toned squares Cut as follows from:
Fabric 6   (1 strip) 13 squares;
Fabric 7   (1 strip) 12 squares;
Fabric 11 (1 strip) 12 squares;
Fabric 12 (1 strip) 10 squares;
Fabric 14 (2 strips) 14 squares;
Fabric 15 (1 strip) 13 squares;
Fabric 16 (1 strip) 12 squares;
Fabric 17 (1 strip) 12 squares;
Fabric 18 (1 strip) 11 squares;
Fabric 19 (1 strip) 12 squares;
Fabric 20 (1 strip) 13 squares;
Fabric 21 (2 strips) 16 squares.
Total of 150 squares.

Backing
From Fabric 22 cut a piece 84in x 74in (213cm x 188cm).

Binding
From Fabric 23 cut 9 strips 2½in (6.4cm) wide across the width of the fabric. Sew together end to end (see page 141).

MAKING THE QUILT
Centre Blocks
The blocks are created with one large dark triangle, two small mid-toned triangles and a fussy-cut square. The blocks measure 10in (25.4cm) finished and are straight set in 6 rows of 5. Use a ¼in (6mm) seam allowance throughout.

Use a design wall and position the patches in the correct layout using the photo and Quilt Assembly Diagram as a guide. Piece 30 blocks, first sewing 2 small mid-toned triangles to a feature square, then sewing that piece to a

FABRIC SWATCH DIAGRAM

Patchwork Fabrics

Fabric 1
SHAGGY
Black
PJ72BK

Fabric 2
LAKE BLOSSOMS
Black
GP93BK

Fabric 3
BIG BLOOMS
Emerald
GP91EM

Fabric 4
CACTUS FLOWER
Black
PJ96BK

Fabric 5
CACTUS FLOWER
Red
PJ96RD

Fabric 6
JUMBLE
Purple
BM53PU

Fabric 7
GOOD VIBRATIONS
Teal
BM65TE

Fabric 8
ROSE AND HYDRANGEA
Blue
PJ97BL

Fabric 9
ROSE AND HYDRANGEA
Navy
PJ97NV

Fabric 10
MILLEFIORE
Dark
GP92DK

Fabric 11
ABORIGINAL DOT
Plum
GP71PL

Fabric 12
ABORIGINAL DOT
Denim
GP71DM

Fabric 13
ABORIGINAL DOT
Orchid
GP71OD

Fabric 14
SPOT
Sapphire
GP70SP

Fabric 15
SPOT
Forest
GP70FO

Fabric 16
SPOT
Green
GP70GN

Fabric 17
SPOT
Purple
GP70PU

Fabric 18
SPOT
Peacock
GP70PC

Fabric 19
SPOT
Royal
GP70RY

Fabric 20
GUINEA FLOWER
Brown
GP59BR

Fabric 21
ONION RINGS
Tomato
BM70TM

Backing and Binding Fabrics

Fabric 22
FRUIT MANDALA
Blue
QB03BL

Fabric 23
SPOT
Black
GP70BK

BLOCK ASSEMBLY DIAGRAM

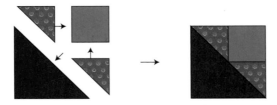

large dark triangle as shown in the Block Assembly Diagram. Sew the blocks together into six rows of five. Taking care to match crossing seams, sew the rows together to complete the quilt centre.

Borders

The borders are made of alternating dark and mid-toned squares, sewn in rows and then sewn together. It is not necessary to place every fabric exactly as in the photo, but lay out all the squares on your design wall, stand back and check there is a good mix of mid-toned colours around the border. Take the top row of 26 squares and sew them together. Then press all seams towards the dark squares. Repeat with the other two top rows and sew the 3 rows together. Complete the bottom border in the same way, then the side borders with 24 squares in each row, also pressing seams towards the dark squares. Sew the side borders to the quilt centre. Press, then finish by sewing the top and bottom borders to the quilt.

FINISHING THE QUILT

Press the quilt top and backing. Layer the quilt top, batting and backing, and baste together (see page 140).
Quilt as desired.
Trim the quilt edges and attach the binding (see page 141).

QUILT ASSEMBLY DIAGRAM

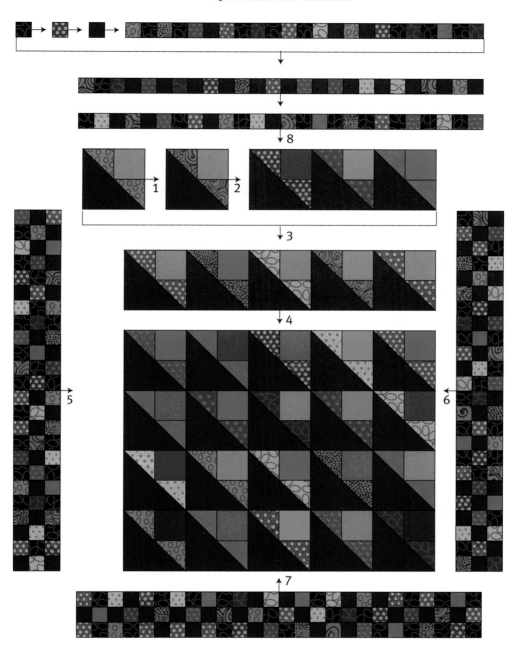

Fabric 1	Fabric 5	Fabric 9	Fabric 13	Fabric 17	Fabric 21
Fabric 2	Fabric 6	Fabric 10	Fabric 14	Fabric 18	
Fabric 3	Fabric 7	Fabric 11	Fabric 15	Fabric 19	
Fabric 4	Fabric 8	Fabric 12	Fabric 16	Fabric 20	

roman tiles *

Kaffe Fassett

This is a tribute to my love of Italian stone floors, like those in St Mark's Cathedral in Venice. The dusty pastel squares really glow in this monochrome setting.

FABRIC SWATCH DIAGRAM

Patchwork Fabrics

Fabric 1
JUMBLE
White
BM53WH

Fabric 2
JUMBLE
Lemon
BM53LE

Fabric 3
JUMBLE
Turquoise
BM53TQ

Fabric 4
JUMBLE
Rose
BM53RO

Fabric 5
JUMBLE
Gold
BM53GD

Fabric 6
JUMBLE
Duck Egg
BM53DE

Fabric 7
SPOT
Charcoal
GP70CC

Fabric 8
SPOT
Teal
GP70TE

Fabric 9
SPOT
White
GP70WH

Fabric 10
SHARK'S TEETH
Blue
BM60BL

Fabric 11
SHARK'S TEETH
Turquoise
BM60TQ

Fabric 12
MAD PLAID
Contrast
BM37CN

Fabric 13
GOOD VIBRATIONS
White
BM65WH

Fabric 14
BANG
Contrast
BM72CN

Fabric 15
BANG
Lavender
BM72LV

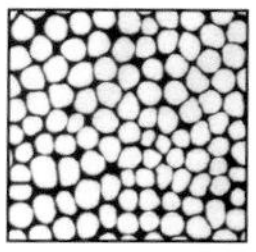

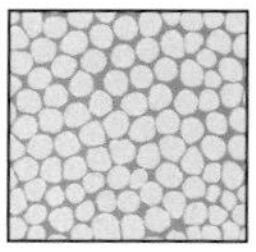

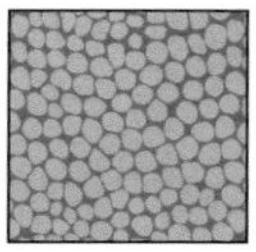

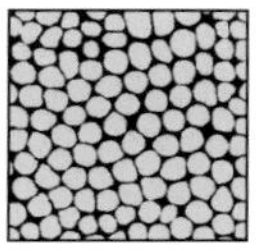

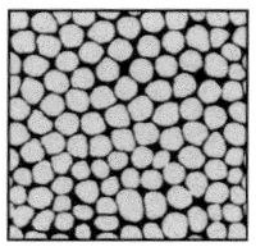

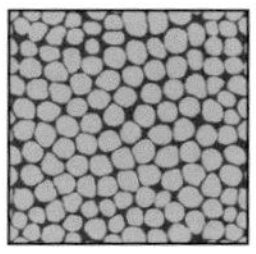

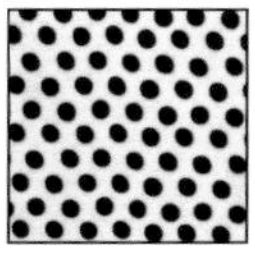

Backing and Binding Fabrics

Fabric 16
PAPER FANS
Contrast
GP143CN

Fabric 17
SPOT
Noir
GP70NO

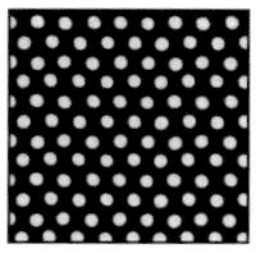

SIZE OF FINISHED QUILT
64½in x 64½in (164cm x 164cm)

FABRICS
Fabrics have been calculated at a maximum width of 40in (102cm), and are cut across the width, unless otherwise stated. Fabrics have been given a number – see Fabric Swatch Diagram for details.

Patchwork Fabrics

JUMBLE			
Fabric 1	White	1½yd (1.4m)
Fabric 2	Lemon	¼yd (25cm)
Fabric 3	Turquoise	¼yd (25cm)
Fabric 4	Rose	¼yd (25cm)
Fabric 5	Gold	¼yd (25cm)
Fabric 6	Duck Egg	¼yd (25cm)

SPOT		
Fabric 7	Charcoal	1⅝yd (1.5m)
Fabric 8	Teal	¼yd (25cm)
Fabric 9	White	⅝yd (60cm)

SHARK'S TEETH		
Fabric 10	Blue	½yd (45cm)
Fabric 11	Turquoise	¼yd (25cm)

MAD PLAID		
Fabric 12	Contrast	⅜yd (40cm)

GOOD VIBRATIONS		
Fabric 13	White	½yd (45cm)

BANG		
Fabric 14	Contrast	¼yd (25cm)
Fabric 15	Lavender	¼yd (25cm)

Backing and Binding Fabrics

PAPER FANS		
Fabric 16	Contrast	4⅛yd (3.8m)

SPOT		
Fabric 17	Noir	⅝yd (60cm)

Batting
73in x 73in (185cm x 185cm)

PATCH SHAPES
All patches are cut from strips cut across the width of the fabric. The split 9-patch block is 12in (30.5cm) square finished and is made using square and half-square triangle (HST) patches, both forming squares 4in x 4in (10.2cm x 10.2cm) finished. The blocks are straight set into rows, as is the border. Use of a design wall will help to lay out the blocks correctly.

CUTTING OUT

Cut strips from the width of the fabric and then cross cut as described.

Half-square Triangle Patches

Cut 4⅞in (12.3cm) strips and cross cut squares 4⅞in (12.3cm). Cut 8 squares from each strip. Cut each square diagonally once to form two half-square triangles (HSTs).
Cut the following squares and HSTs:
Fabric 1 (5 strips) 36 squares, 72 HSTs;
Fabric 7 (6 strips) 46 squares, 92 HSTs;
Fabric 9 (3 strips) 20 squares, 40 HSTs;
Fabric 10 (2 strips) 16 squares, 32 HSTs;
Fabric 12 (1 strip) 3 squares, 6 HSTs*;
Fabric 13 (3 strips) 23 squares, 46 HSTs);
* Note: Use remaining fabric for squares

Square Patches

Cut 4½in (11.4cm) strips and cross cut squares 4½in (11.4cm). Cut 8 squares from each strip.
Cut the following squares:
Fabric 1 (5 strips) 36 squares;
Fabric 2 (1 strip) 2 squares;
Fabric 3 (1 strip) 2 squares;
Fabric 4 (1 strip) 2 squares;
Fabric 5 (1 strip) 1 square;
Fabric 6 (1 strip) 1 square;
Fabric 7 (5 strips) 39 squares;
Fabric 8 (1 strip) 2 squares;
Fabric 9 (1 strip) 6 squares;
Fabric 10 (1 strip) 6 squares;
Fabric 11 (1 strip) 2 squares;
Fabric 12 (1 strip) 9 squares*:
Fabric 14 (1 strip) 2 squares;
Fabric 15 (1 strip) 2 squares.
* Note: Use remaining fabric from triangles

Backing

From Fabric 16 remove selvedges and cut one piece of fabric 40in x 73in (102cm x 185cm) and one piece 34in x 73in (84cm x 185cm).

Binding

From Fabric 17 cut 7 strips 2½in (6.4cm). Sew end to end (see page 141).

MAKING THE QUILT

Use a ¼in (6mm) seam allowance throughout. Where possible press the seams toward the dark fabric.

Making the Centre Blocks

Referring to the Block Assembly Diagram, take 3 matching light, 3 matching dark and 1 colour square patches plus 2 matching light and 2 matching dark HST patches. Sew the light and dark triangles together along their long edge to make 2 squares (a). Arrange the pieced squares with the other patches as shown in (b) and sew together in rows, then sew the rows together, matching seam joins, to create the finished block (c). Make 16 blocks.
Using the Quilt Assembly Diagram as a guide, arrange the blocks so the dark halves are in the same position and sew the blocks together in rows of 4. Press seams and sew the 4 rows together.

Making the Borders

Arrange the patches using the same dark and light method as the blocks. Referring to the Quilt Assembly Diagram, sew one dark and one light triangle together to make a square. Ensuring the dark and light triangles all face the same way as the centre blocks, sew 4 rows of 12 squares for the top and bottom borders. Sew 2 rows of 12 together, then sew the top and bottom borders to the quilt centre. Sew 4 rows of 16 squares for the side borders. Sew 2 rows of 16 together for each side, then sew the two side borders to the quilt.

FINISHING THE QUILT

Sew the 2 backing pieces together using a ¼in (6mm) seam allowance to form a piece approx. 73in x 73in (185cm x 185cm). Layer the quilt top, batting and backing, and baste together (see page 140).
Quilt as desired.
Trim the quilt edges and attach the binding (see page 141).

BLOCK ASSEMBLY DIAGRAM

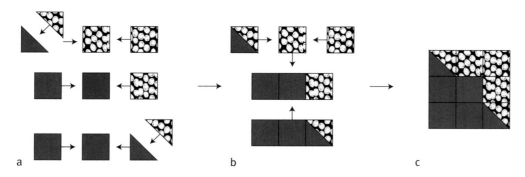

QUILT ASSEMBLY DIAGRAM

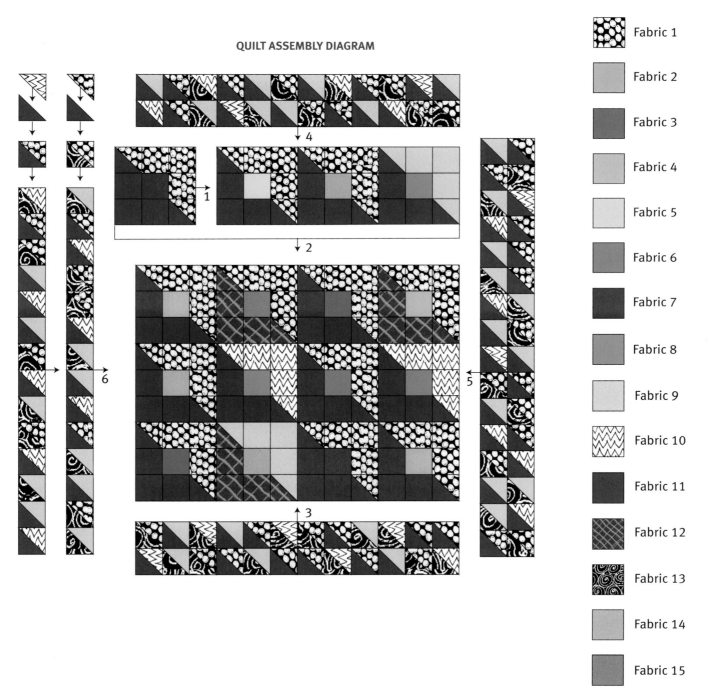

Fabric 1
Fabric 2
Fabric 3
Fabric 4
Fabric 5
Fabric 6
Fabric 7
Fabric 8
Fabric 9
Fabric 10
Fabric 11
Fabric 12
Fabric 13
Fabric 14
Fabric 15

diamond carpet ***

Kaffe Fassett

This Trip Around the World quilt is inspired by the workshops I've given where my students have been exploring a black and white theme with exciting results, so this quilt design is an homage to their creativity. In this cool interpretation (of the *Jubilee Garden* design from *A Colourful Journey*) the diamonds are laid out in concentric layers and then sewn together in diagonal rows.

SIZE OF FINISHED QUILT
91½in x 96½in (233cm x 245cm)

FABRICS
Fabrics have been calculated at a maximum width of 40in (102cm), and are cut across the width, unless otherwise stated. Fabrics have been given a number – see Fabric Swatch Diagram for details.

Patchwork Fabrics
GEODES
Fabric 1   Grey   1yd (90cm)
Fabric 2   Blue   1yd (90cm)
SPOT
Fabric 3   Charcoal   ⅛yd (15cm)
* see also Binding Fabric
Fabric 4   White   1yd (90cm)
VARIEGATED MORNING GLORY
Fabric 5   Aqua   ½yd (45cm)
BANG
Fabric 6   Lavender   ¾ yd (70cm)
Fabric 7   Contrast   ½yd (45cm)
CHIPS
Fabric 8   White   1¼yd (1.2m)
JUMBLE
Fabric 9   White   ¾yd (70cm)
Fabric 10   Duck Egg   ½yd (45cm)
Fabric 11   Turquoise   ½yd (45cm)
ONION RINGS
Fabric 12   Black   ½yd (45cm)
SHARK'S TEETH
Fabric 13   Blue   ½yd (45cm)
GUINEA FLOWER
Fabric 14   Blue   1¼yd (1.2m)
PAPER FANS
Fabric 15   Delft   ¾yd (70cm)

Backing and Binding Fabrics
GUINEA FLOWER
Fabric 14   Blue   8¾yd (8m)
SPOT
Fabric 3   Charcoal   ¾yd (70cm)
* see also Patchwork Fabrics

Batting
100in x 105in (254cm x 267cm)

FABRIC SWATCH DIAGRAM

Patchwork Fabrics

Fabric 1
GEODES
Grey
PJ99GY

Fabric 2
GEODES
Blue
PJ99BL

Fabric 3
SPOT
Charcoal
GP70CC

Fabric 4
SPOT
White
GP70WH

Fabric 5
VARIEGATED MORNING GLORY
Aqua
PJ98AQ

Fabric 6
BANG
Lavender
BM72LV

Fabric 7
BANG
Contrast
BM72CN

Fabric 8
CHIPS
White
BM73WH

Fabric 9
JUMBLE
White
BM53WH

Fabric 10
JUMBLE
Duck Egg
BM53DE

Fabric 11
JUMBLE
Turquoise
BM53TQ

Fabric 12
ONION RINGS
Black
BM70BK

Fabric 13
SHARK'S TEETH
Blue
BM60BL

Fabric 14
GUINEA FLOWER
Blue
GP59BL

Fabric 15
PAPER FANS
Delft
GP143DT

Backing and Binding Fabrics

Fabric 14
GUINEA FLOWER
Blue
GP59BL

Fabric 3
SPOT
Charcoal
GP70CC

PATCH SHAPES

The quilt is made up of the following 60° diamond and 60° triangle patch shapes all with 3½in (8.9cm) sides (see Templates on pages 136–137): diamond patch (Template A); triangle (Template B) for top and bottom rows; half-triangle (Template C and C Reverse) for the corners; and half-diamond (Template D) for the sides. Cut patches from 3½in (8.9cm) strips using templates or a 60° triangle ruler. (If your ruler has a top point, position it just off the top of the fabric strip when cutting.)

TEMPLATES

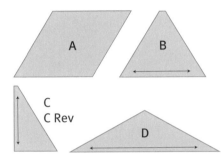

CUTTING OUT

Diamonds, Triangles and Half-triangles
Cut strips 3½in (8.9cm) wide and using Templates A, B or C/C Reverse as required, cross cut the required pieces. Nine diamonds can be cut from each strip and a Triangle B can be cut from the end of each row of diamonds, if required.
Template A diamonds Use Method 1 for odd rows and use Method 2 for even rows to ensure the bias edges are matched to straight-grain edges, thus stabilizing the joined patches. Diamonds can be cut using either a ruler or a template. If using a template, flip it over to cut the even row (Method 2) diamonds.
From the following fabrics, cut strips and cross cut as follows:

CUTTING DIAGRAM

Method 1: Odd rows

Method 2: Even rows

Fabric 1 – Method 1 (9 strips)
55 Diamond A, 34 Triangle B;
Fabric 2 – Method 1 (9 strips)
78 Diamond A, 4 Triangle B;
Fabric 3 – Method 2 (1 strip)
4 Diamond A;
Fabric 4 – Method 2 (8 strips)
72 Diamond A;
Fabric 5 – Method 1 (5 strips)
38 Diamond A, 4 Triangle B;
Fabric 6 – Method 1 (6 strips)
46 Diamond A, 4 Triangle B, 2 Half-triangle C and 2 Half-triangle C Reverse;
Fabric 7 – Method 1 (4 strips)
32 Diamond A;
Fabric 8 – Method 2 (12 strips)
104 Diamond A;
Fabric 9 – Method 2 (7 strips)
60 Diamond A;
Fabric 10 – Method 1 (4 strips)
34 Diamond A, 4 Triangle B;
Fabric 11 – Method 1 (4 strips)
36 Diamond A;
Fabric 12 – Method 2 (4 strips)
34 Diamond A;
Fabric 13 – Method 2 (4 strips)
34 Diamond A;
Fabric 14 – Method 2 (12 strips)
108 Diamond A;
Fabric 15 – Method 1 (7 strips)
56 Diamond A.

Side Half-diamonds
From Fabric 6, cut 4 strips 2¼in (5.7cm) wide. Using Template D, cut 9 side half-diamonds from each strip, rotating the template 180° after each cut. 30 in total.

Backing
Cut 3 pieces, each 100in (254cm) long, remove selvedges and sew together to make a backing approximately 100in x120in (254cm x 305cm). Trim down to 100in x 108in (254in x 274cm).

Binding
From Fabric 3 cut 10 strips 2½in (6.4cm) wide. Sew end to end (see page 141).

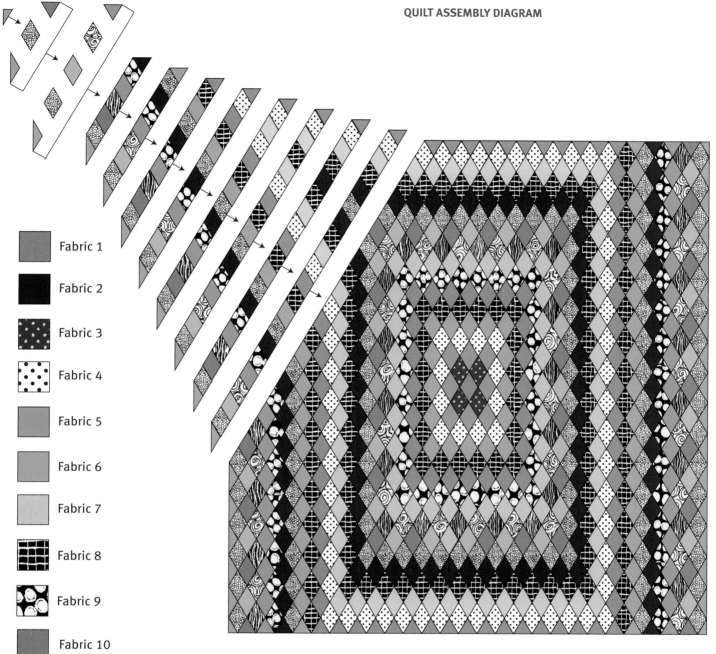

Fabric 1

Fabric 2

Fabric 3

Fabric 4

Fabric 5

Fabric 6

Fabric 7

Fabric 8

Fabric 9

Fabric 10

Fabric 11

Fabric 12

Fabric 13

Fabric 14

Fabric 15

MAKING THE QUILT

Lay out the pieces using the photograph and Quilt Assembly Diagram as guides, starting in the centre and working outwards. Fill in the top and bottom edges of the quilt with the corresponding triangles, and the sides with the side half-diamonds. Complete the layout with 2 half-triangle pieces and 2 half-triangle reverse pieces in the corners.

Using a ¼in (6mm) seam allowance throughout, sew the pieces together in diagonal rows as shown in the Quilt Assembly Diagram.

FINISHING THE QUILT

Layer the quilt top, batting and backing, and baste together (see page 140). Quilt as desired.
Trim the quilt edges and attach the binding (see page 141).

fruits of the forest **

Kaffe Fassett

The scale changes in this pinwheel quilt make it very lively to my eye. I used some contrast in the palette to show off more clearly the delightful triangle structure.

SIZE OF FINISHED QUILT
80½in x 80½in (204cm x 204cm)

FABRICS
Fabrics have been calculated at a maximum width of 40in (102cm), and are cut across the width, unless otherwise stated. Fabrics have been given a number – see Fabric Swatch Diagram for details.

Patchwork Fabrics
OMBRE LEAVES
Fabric 1	Purple	¼yd (25cm)
Fabric 2	Pink	1⅜yd (1.3m)
Fabric 3	Blue	¼yd (25cm)

* see also Backing Fabric
SPOT
Fabric 4	Black	⅝yd (60cm)
Fabric 5	Violet	¼yd (25cm)

ABORIGINAL DOT
Fabric 6	Shocking	¼yd (25cm)

ONION RINGS
Fabric 7	Cocoa	⅝yd (60cm)

BALI BROCADE
Fabric 8	Purple	2⅛yd (2m)

ORANGES
Fabric 9	Purple	⅝yd (60cm)

GUINEA FLOWER
Fabric 10	Pink	1¼yd (1.2m)

MOSAIC CIRCLES
Fabric 11	Pink	⅝yd (60cm)

Backing and Binding Fabrics
OMBRE LEAVES
Fabric 3	Blue	5¾yd (5.3m)

* see also Patchwork Fabrics
JUMBLE
Fabric 12	Blue	¾yd (70cm)

Batting
89in x 89in (226cm x 226cm)

PATCH SHAPES
This medallion quilt has three borders of pinwheels around a central pinwheel block. It is made using three sizes of pinwheel blocks with finished sizes of 6in (15.2cm) – small, 12in (30.5cm) – medium and 16in (40.6cm) – large. All patches are squares cut from strips, cut diagonally into half-square triangles

FABRIC SWATCH DIAGRAM

Patchwork Fabrics

Fabric 1
OMBRE LEAVES
Purple
GP174PU

Fabric 2
OMBRE LEAVES
Pink
GP174PK

Fabric 3
OMBRE LEAVES
Blue
GP174BL

Fabric 4
SPOT
Black
GP70BK

Fabric 5
SPOT
Violet
GP70VI

Fabric 6
ABORIGINAL DOT
Shocking
GP71SG

Fabric 7
ONION RINGS
Cocoa
BM70CO

Fabric 8
BALI BROCADE
Purple
BM69PU

Fabric 9
ORANGES
Purple
GP177PU

Fabric 10
GUINEA FLOWER
Pink
GP59PK

Fabric 11
MOSAIC CIRCLES
Pink
GP176PK

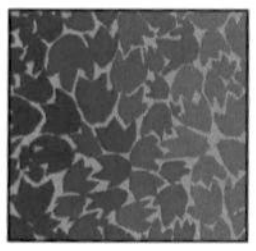

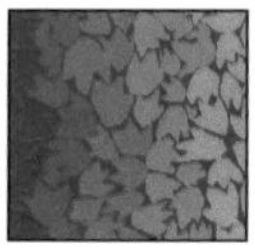

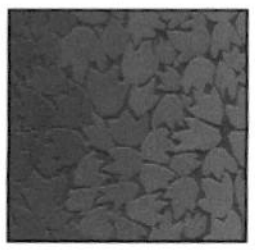

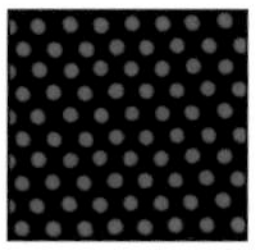

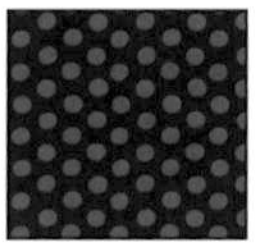

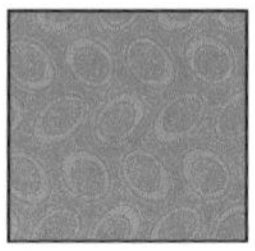

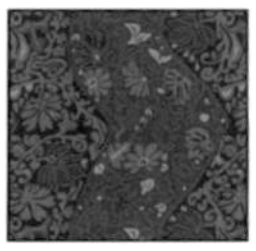

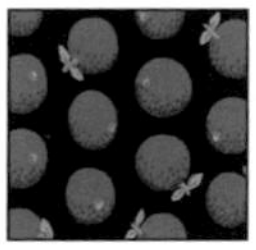

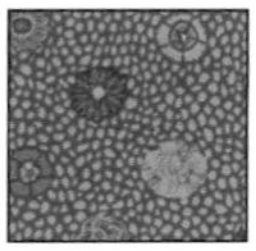

Backing and Binding Fabrics

Fabric 3
OMBRE LEAVES
Blue
GP174BL

Fabric 12
JUMBLE
Blue
BM53BL

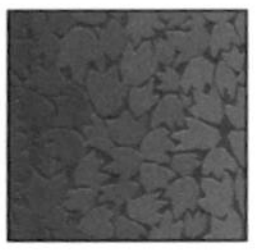

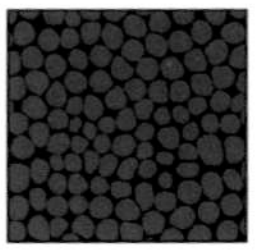

(HSTs) and sewn together to make squares. Correct placement of the light and dark fabrics, and correct orientation of the triangles, is important to the overall pinwheel effect.

CUTTING OUT
Cut the fabric in strips across the width of the fabric then cross cut as described.

Border 3 – Large Pinwheel Blocks
Cut strips 8⅞in (22.5cm) wide and cross cut squares 8⅞in (22.5cm). 4 squares can be cut from each strip. Cut each square diagonally once to make 2 HSTs from each square.
Cut from the following fabrics:
Fabric 2 (4 strips) 16 squares, 32 HSTs;
Fabric 8 (8 strips) 32 squares, 64 HSTs;
Fabric 10 (4 strips) 16 squares, 32 HSTs.

Centre and Border 2 – Medium Pinwheel Blocks
Cut strips 6⅞in (17.5cm) wide and cross cut squares 6⅞in (17.5cm). 5 squares can be cut from each strip. Cut each square diagonally once to make 2 HSTs from each square.

Cut from the following fabrics:
Fabric 1 (1 strip) 2 squares, 4 HSTs;
Fabric 4 (3 strips) 14 squares, 28 HSTs;
Fabric 7 (3 strips) 12 squares, 24 HSTs;
Fabric 9 (3 strips) 12 squares, 24 HSTs;
Fabric 11 (3 strips) 12 squares, 24 HSTs.

Border 1 – Small Pinwheel Blocks
Cut strips 3⅞in (9.8cm) wide and cross cut squares 3⅞in (9.8cm). 10 squares can be cut from each strip. Cut each square diagonally once to make 2 HSTs from each square. Cut 2 strips and then cross cut 12 squares from each of the following fabrics:
Fabric 2 (2 strips) 12 squares, 24 HSTs;
Fabric 3 (2 strips) 12 squares, 24 HSTs;
Fabric 5 (2 strips) 12 squares, 24 HSTs;
Fabric 6 (2 strips) 12 squares, 24 HSTs.

Backing
From Fabric 3 cut two pieces 40in x 89in (102cm x 226cm).
From the remaining fabric, remove the selvedges and cut 4 strips down the length of the fabric 22¾in (57.8cm) long and 10in (25.4cm) wide. Sew the 4 pieces end to end to create a strip measuring 10in x 89in (25.4cm x 226cm). Sew the 3 backing pieces together to make a piece approx. 89in x 89in (226cm x 226cm).

Binding
From Fabric 12 cut 9 strips 2½in (6.4cm) across the width of the fabric. Sew together end to end (see page 141).

MAKING THE BLOCKS
Use ¼in (6mm) seams throughout and refer to the Quilt Assembly Diagram for fabric placement. Using a design wall will help correct placement of pieces and blocks.
The pinwheel blocks are all made in the same way. Sew a light and dark HST together down the long edge to form a square, press, sew 2 squares together ensuring the HST points are positioned correctly to form the pinwheel pattern, then sew 2 pairs of squares together to complete the pinwheel block. Refer to Block Assembly Diagrams A and B and the Finished Block Diagram C.
Note: To reduce bulk at the centre of the blocks, press the centre point seams open.

Centre Make a medium 12in (30.5cm) pinwheel block.

Border 1 Make 12 small 6in (15.2cm) pinwheel blocks.

Border 2 Make 12 medium 12in (30.5cm) pinwheel blocks.

Border 3 Make 16 large 16in (40.6cm) pinwheel blocks.

MAKING THE QUILT

Lay out all the quilt blocks on a design wall to check block placement.

Centre and Border 1 Sew 2 small pinwheel blocks together and sew to the top and bottom of the centre block. Sew 4 small pinwheel blocks together and sew to each side of the centre block.

Border 2 Sew 2 medium pinwheel blocks together and sew to the top and bottom of the quilt. Sew 4 medium pinwheel blocks together and sew to each side of the quilt.

Border 3 Sew 3 large pinwheel blocks together and sew to the top and bottom of the quilt. Sew 5 large pinwheel blocks together and sew to each side of the quilt.

FINISHING THE QUILT

Press the quilt top. Layer the quilt top, batting and backing, and baste together (see page 140).

Quilt as desired.

Trim the quilt edges and attach the binding (see page 141).

BLOCK ASSEMBLY DIAGRAM

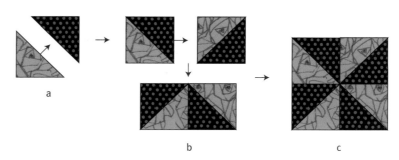

a   b   c

QUILT ASSEMBLY DIAGRAM

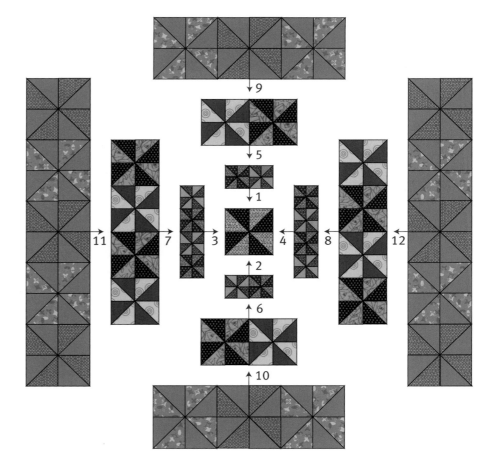

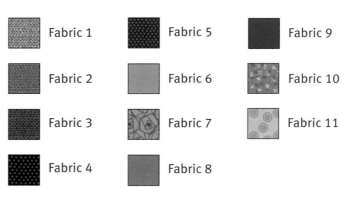

Fabric 1	Fabric 5	Fabric 9
Fabric 2	Fabric 6	Fabric 10
Fabric 3	Fabric 7	Fabric 11
Fabric 4	Fabric 8	

geometric snowballs **

Kaffe Fassett

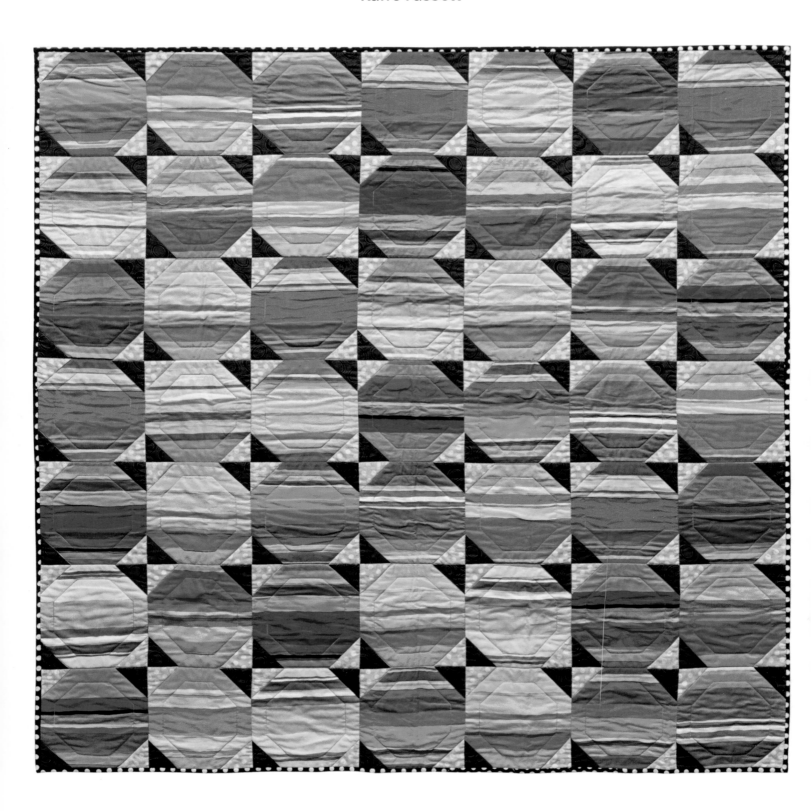

Taking four different colourways of my new Promenade Stripe produced this very dramatic quilt, full of movement. The dark and light corners echo the white frames around so many of the houses in Burano.

FABRIC SWATCH DIAGRAM

Patchwork Fabrics

Fabric 1
PROMENADE STRIPE
Contrast
GP178CN

Fabric 2
PROMENADE STRIPE
Cold
GP178CD

Fabric 3
PROMENADE STRIPE
Sunny
GP178SY

Fabric 4
PROMENADE STRIPE
Hot
GP178HT

Fabric 5
SPOT
Silver
GP70SV

Fabric 6
ABORIGINAL DOT
Orchid
GP71OD

Backing and Binding Fabrics

Fabric 7
BANG
Yellow
BM72YE

Fabric 8
SPOT
Noir
GP70NO

SIZE OF FINISHED QUILT
53in x 53in (135cm x 135cm)

FABRICS
Fabrics have been calculated at a maximum width of 40in (102cm), and are cut across the width, unless otherwise stated. Fabrics have been given a number – see Fabric Swatch Diagram for details.

Patchwork Fabrics
PROMENADE STRIPE

Fabric 1	Contrast	¾yd (70cm)
Fabric 2	Cold	½yd (45cm)
Fabric 3	Sunny	¾yd (70cm)
Fabric 4	Hot	¾yd (70cm)

SPOT

Fabric 5	Silver	⅝yd (60cm)

ABORIGINAL DOT

Fabric 6	Orchid	⅝yd (60cm)

Backing and Binding Fabrics
BANG

Fabric 7	Yellow	3½yd (3.3m)

SPOT

Fabric 8	Noir	½yd (45cm)

Batting
61in x 61in (155cm x 155cm)

PATCH SHAPES
The quilt is made up with traditional octagonal snowball blocks. They are made the easy way using 1 large square (with the stripe running horizontally) and 4 small squares for each block; two fabrics are used for the small squares, placed diagonally in the same position for each block. They are sewn diagonally across the corner, trimmed and flipped back to replace the corners of the large square.

CUTTING OUT
All the patch shapes are cut from strips cut across the width of the fabric and cross cut into squares. Don't try to match sections of stripes to the original pieces.

Block Centres
Cut 8in (20.3cm) strips across the width of the fabric and cross cut 8in (20.3cm) squares. Each strip will give 5 squares. Cut a total of 49 squares from the following fabrics:
Fabric 1 (3 strips) 11 squares;
Fabric 2 (2 strips) 10 squares;
Fabric 3 (3 strips) 13 squares;
Fabric 4 (3 strips) 15 squares.

Block Corners
Cut 2¾in (7cm) strips across the width of the fabric and cross cut 2¾in (7cm) squares. Each strip will give 14 squares. Cut strips and squares as follows:
Fabric 5 (7 strips) 98 squares;
Fabric 6 (7 strips) 98 squares.

Backing
From Fabric 7 cut 1 piece 40in x 61in (102cm x 155cm) and 1 piece 21½in x 61in (54.6cm x 155cm).

Binding
From Fabric 8 cut 6 strips 2½in (6.4cm) wide across the width of the fabric and sew together end to end (see page 141).

MAKING THE SNOWBALL BLOCKS
Take 1 large square with the stripes running horizontally, 2 small squares in Fabric 5 and 2 small squares in Fabric 6. Following the sequence in the Block Assembly Diagram, place the 4 small squares right sides together on to the large square making sure the 2 fabrics are in diagonal pairs and in the same position on each large square. Matching the edges carefully, stitch diagonally across the small squares as shown (a) and trim the corners to a ¼in (6mm) seam allowance (b). Press the corners outwards (c). Make 49 blocks in total.

BLOCK ASSEMBLY DIAGRAM

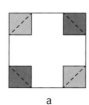

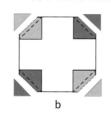

a   b   c

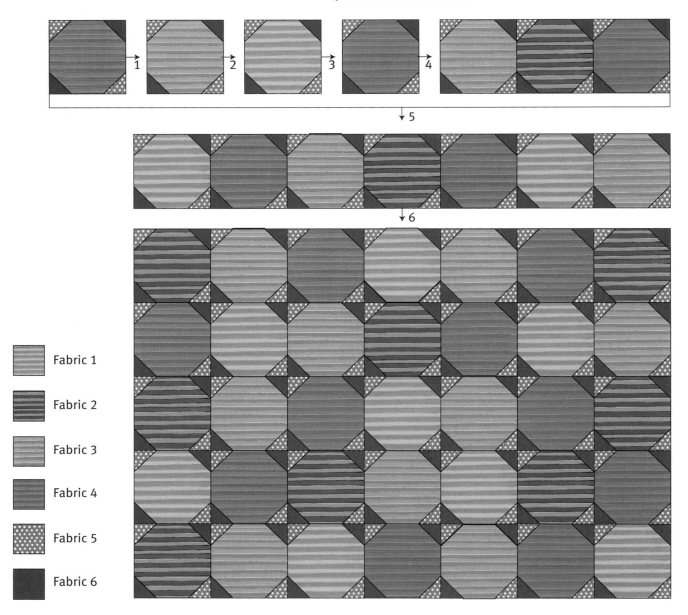

Fabric 1

Fabric 2

Fabric 3

Fabric 4

Fabric 5

Fabric 6

MAKING THE QUILT

Use a ¼in (6mm) seam allowance throughout. Lay out the blocks as shown in the Quilt Assembly Diagram. Sew into rows of 7 blocks and press seams in opposite directions for alternating rows. Sew the 7 rows together, carefully matching seam joins.

FINISHING THE QUILT

Press the quilt top. Sew the backing pieces together using a ¼in (6mm) seam allowance to form a backing piece 61in x 61in (155cm x 155cm).
Layer the quilt top, batting and backing, and baste together (see page 140).
Quilt as desired.
Trim the quilt edges and attach the binding (see page 141).

succulent *

Kaffe Fassett

When I was growing up in California, succulent gardens were a great favourite of mine. They had a limited palette of silvery greens that drew attention to the wonderful shapes of the plants. This cool arrangement has the same watery appeal.

SIZE OF FINISHED QUILT
Approx. 84½in x 84½in (215cm x 215cm)

FABRICS
Fabrics have been calculated at a maximum width of 40in (102cm), and are cut across the width, unless otherwise stated. Fabrics have been given a number – see Fabric Swatch Diagram for details.

Patchwork Fabrics
SPOT

Fabric 1	China Blue	⅜yd (40cm)
Fabric 2	Duck Egg	⅜yd (40cm)
Fabric 3	Green	½yd (45cm)
Fabric 4	Guava	⅜yd (40cm)
Fabric 5	Teal	¼yd (25cm)
Fabric 6	Turquoise	½yd (45cm)

JUMBLE

Fabric 7	Turquoise	⅜yd (40cm)

*see also Binding Fabric (overleaf)

Fabric 8	Duck Egg	⅜yd (40cm)

BRASSICA

Fabric 9	Green	⅜yd (40cm)

PAPERWEIGHT

Fabric 10	Algae	¼yd (25cm)

ROMAN GLASS

Fabric 11	Emerald	⅜yd (40cm)

SHARK'S TEETH

Fabric 12	Turquoise	⅜yd (40cm)

CATERPILLAR STRIPE

Fabric 13	Blue	⅜yd (40cm)

MILLEFIORE

Fabric 14	Jade	⅜yd (40cm)

JUPITER

Fabric 15	Malachite	½yd (45cm)

PAPER FANS

Fabric 16	Delft	⅜yd (40cm)

STONE FLOWER

Fabric 17	Turquoise	⅜yd (40cm)
Fabric 18	Lavender	½yd (45cm)

CACTUS FLOWER

Fabric 19	Green	⅜yd (40cm)

ENCHANTED

Fabric 20	Green	⅝yd (60cm)

PRIMULAS

Fabric 21	Periwinkle	⅜yd (40cm)

ROSE AND HYDRANGEA

Fabric 22	Green	⅜yd (40cm)

BALI BROCADE

Fabric 23	Contrast	4½yd (4.2m)

if fussy cut down the length of the fabric; if cut across the fabric width 1½yd (1.4m)

FABRIC SWATCH DIAGRAM

Patchwork Fabrics

Fabric 1
SPOT
China Blue
GP70CI

Fabric 2
SPOT
Duck Egg
GP70DE

Fabric 3
SPOT
Green
GP70GN

Fabric 4
SPOT
Guava
GP70GU

Fabric 5
SPOT
Teal
GP70TE

Fabric 6
SPOT
Turquoise
GP70TQ

Fabric 7
JUMBLE
Turquoise
BM53TQ

Fabric 8
JUMBLE
Duck Egg
BM53DE

Fabric 9
BRASSICA
Green
PJ51GN

Fabric 10
PAPERWEIGHT
Algae
GP20AG

Fabric 11
ROMAN GLASS
Emerald
GP01EM

Fabric 12
SHARK'S TEETH
Turquoise
BM60TQ

Fabric 13
CATERPILLAR STRIPE
Blue
WCATBL

Fabric 14
MILLEFIORE
Jade
GP92JA

Fabric 15
JUPITER
Malachite
GP131MA

Fabric 16
PAPER FANS
Delft
GP143DF

Fabric 17
STONE FLOWER
Turquoise
GP173TQ

Fabric 18
STONE FLOWER
Lavender
GP173LV

Fabric 19
CACTUS FLOWER
Green
PJ96GN

Fabric 20
ENCHANTED
Green
GP172GN

Fabric 21
PRIMULAS
Periwinkle
BM71PE

Fabric 22
ROSE AND HYDRANGEA
Green
PJ097GN

Fabric 23
BALI BROCADE
Contrast
BM069CN

Backing and Binding Fabrics

Fabric 24
DREAM
Blue
GP148BL

Fabric 7
JUMBLE
Turquoise
BM53TQ

Backing and Binding Fabrics
DREAM
Fabric 24   Blue   6½yd (6m)
JUMBLE
Fabric 7   Turquoise   ¾yd (70cm)
* see also Patchwork Fabrics

Batting
93in x 93in (236cm x 236cm)

PATCHES
Rows of 4-patch blocks alternating with rows of a mixture of large feature squares and 4-patch blocks, make up the quilt top. Blocks are 8in (20.3cm) square finished.

CUTTING OUT
Cut fabrics across the width of the fabric and cross cut as described.

Large Feature Squares
Cut a strip 8½in (21.6cm) and cross cut 8½in (21.6cm) squares. Each strip will give you 4 squares.
Cut 16 large squares – 4 from each of the following: Fabric 19; Fabric 20; Fabric 21; Fabric 22.

Small Squares
Cut strips 4½in (11.4cm) wide across the width of the fabric and cross cut 4½in (11.4cm) squares. Each strip will give you 8 squares. Cut 260 small squares as follows:
Fabric 1 (2 strips) 11 squares;
Fabric 2 (2 strips) 11 squares;
Fabric 3 (3 strips) 23 squares;
Fabric 4 (2 strips) 14 squares;
Fabric 5 (1 strip) 8 squares;
Fabric 6 (3 strips) 17 squares;
Fabric 7 (2 strips) 15 squares;
Fabric 8 (2 strips) 16 squares;
Fabric 9 (2 strips) 13 squares;
Fabric 10 (1 strip) 8 squares;
Fabric 11 (2 strips) 13 squares;
Fabric 12 (2 strips) 16 squares;
Fabric 13 (2 strips) 11 squares;
Fabric 14 (2 strips) 16 squares;
Fabric 15 (3 strips) 17 squares;
Fabric 16 (2 strips) 11 squares;
Fabric 17 (2 strips) 10 squares;
Fabric 18 (3 strips) 18 squares;
Fabric 20 (2 strips) 12 squares.

BLOCK ASSEMBLY DIAGRAM

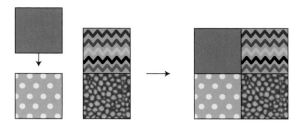

Borders
Borders are fussy cut down the length of the fabric, parallel to the selvedge, to use the paler area of Fabric 23. You will be able to cut 2 strips from each full length of fabric.
From Fabric 23 cut 1 length 84½in (214.6cm) long and from that length cut 2 strips 6½in (16.5cm) wide along the pale grey sections of the fabric.
Cut 1 length 72½in (184.1cm) long and from that length cut 2 strips 6½in (16.5cm) wide along the pale grey sections of the fabric.

Backing
Remove selvedges from Fabric 24. Cut 2 pieces 93in (236cm) long and 1 piece 47in (119cm) long. Cut the shorter piece in half down its length and sew together end to end. Sew the 3 pieces together to form a piece 93in x 93in (236cm x 236cm).

Binding
From Fabric 7 cut 9 strips 2½in (6.4cm) wide across the width of the fabric and sew together end to end (see page 141).

MAKING THE QUILT
Use a ¼in (6mm) seam allowance throughout, and refer to the Block Assembly Diagram and Quilt Assembly Diagram for construction and fabric placement.

Quilt Centre
Piece 65 4-patch blocks made up of 2 light and 2 medium squares, referring to the Block Assembly Diagram. Use a design wall to lay out the quilt, forming alternating rows. The first row is 9

4-square blocks and the second row is alternating 4-square blocks and large feature squares. Use the photograph and Quilt Assembly Diagram to help with block placement. Sew the blocks and large squares together to form 9 rows. Sew the 9 rows together to complete the centre.

Borders
Pin and sew the shorter 72½in (184.1cm) borders to each side of the quilt top, then pin and sew the longer 84½in (214.6cm) borders to the top and bottom to complete the quilt top.

FINISHING THE QUILT
Press the quilt top. Layer the quilt top, batting and backing, and baste together (see page 140).
Quilt as desired.
Trim the quilt edges and attach the binding (see page 141).

QUILT ASSEMBLY DIAGRAM

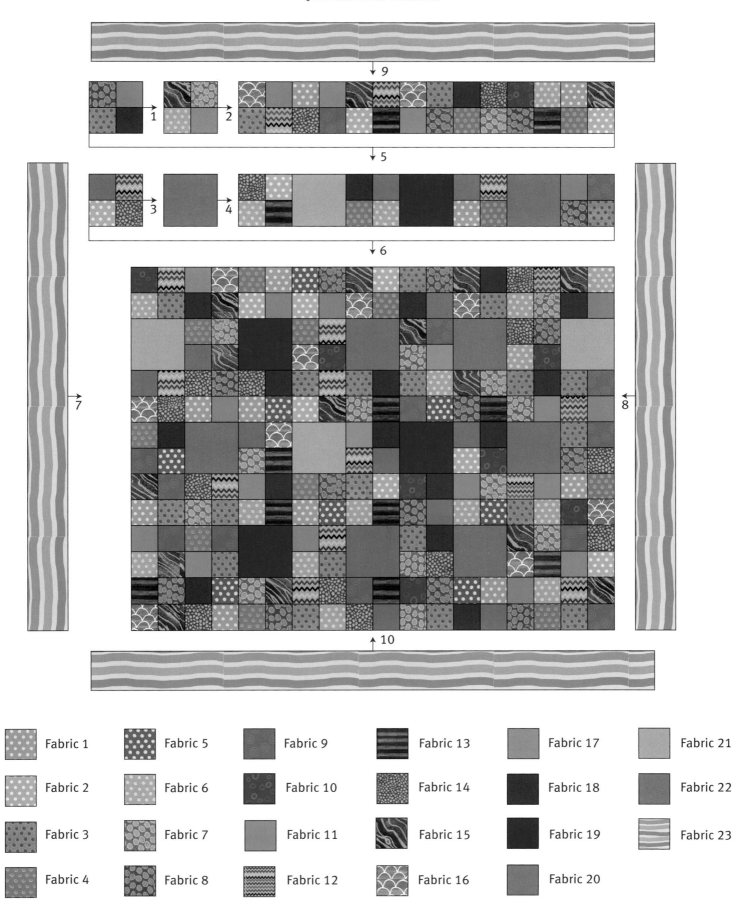

Fabric 1
Fabric 5
Fabric 9
Fabric 13
Fabric 17
Fabric 21

Fabric 2
Fabric 6
Fabric 10
Fabric 14
Fabric 18
Fabric 22

Fabric 3
Fabric 7
Fabric 11
Fabric 15
Fabric 19
Fabric 23

Fabric 4
Fabric 8
Fabric 12
Fabric 16
Fabric 20

honeycomb ∗∗∗

Kaffe Fassett

An Indian textile that I liked inspired the variations of squares that make this so intriguing. The spice market colours give it a warm exotic feel too.

SIZE OF FINISHED QUILT
78½in x 78½in (200cm x 200cm)

FABRICS
Fabrics have been calculated at a maximum width of 40in (102cm), and are cut across the width, unless otherwise stated. Fabrics have been given a number – see Fabric Swatch Diagram for details.

Patchwork Fabrics
JUMBLE		
Fabric 1	Tangerine	1¾yd (1.7m)
ABORIGINAL DOT		
Fabric 2	Orchid	1yd (90cm)
Fabric 3	Orange	1yd (90cm)
SPOT		
Fabric 4	Ochre	¼yd (25cm)
Fabric 5	Magenta	½yd (45cm)

* see also Binding Fabric
Fabric 6	Violet	1yd (90cm)
Fabric 7	Gold	1¼yd (1.2m)
Fabric 8	Purple	¼yd (25cm)
Fabric 9	Orange	⅛yd (15cm)
SHARK'S TEETH		
Fabric 10	Orange	⅝yd (60cm)
CHIPS		
Fabric 11	Charcoal	⅝yd (60cm)

Backing and Binding Fabrics
SEA URCHINS		
Fabric 12	Antique	7¼yd (6.7m)
SPOT		
Fabric 5	Magenta	¾yd (70cm)

* see also Patchwork Fabrics

Batting
87in x 87in (221cm x 221cm)

PATCH SHAPES
There are 7 different log cabin blocks (A, B, C, D, E, F and G) used to make up the quilt. Each round of strips (logs) has two lengths – shorter lengths are sewn on opposite sides, then longer lengths on the remaining 2 sides. Three further blocks (H, J and K) are used to make the side and corner setting part-blocks. Blocks are set on point in rows of 3 or 4 blocks with H, J or K part-blocks

FABRIC SWATCH DIAGRAM

Patchwork Fabrics

Fabric 1
JUMBLE
Tangerine
BM53TN

Fabric 2
ABORIGINAL DOT
Orchid
GP71OD

Fabric 3
ABORIGINAL DOT
Orange
GP71OR

Fabric 4
SPOT
Ochre
GP70OC

Fabric 5
SPOT
Magenta
GP70MG

Fabric 6
SPOT
Violet
GP70VI

Fabric 7
SPOT
Gold
GP70GD

Fabric 8
SPOT
Purple
GP70PU

Fabric 9
SPOT
Orange
GP70OR

Fabric 10
SHARK'S TEETH
Orange
BM60OR

Fabric 11
CHIPS
Charcoal
BM73CC

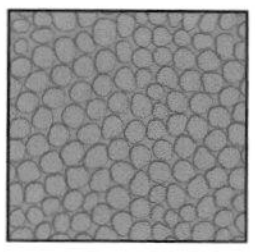

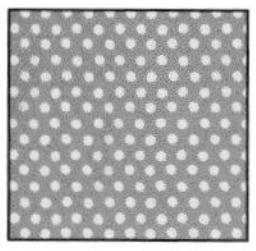

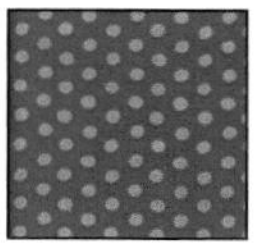

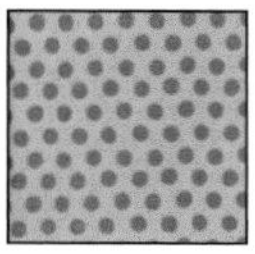

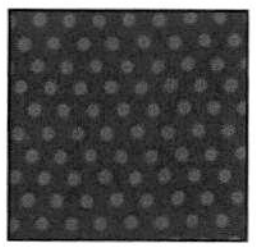

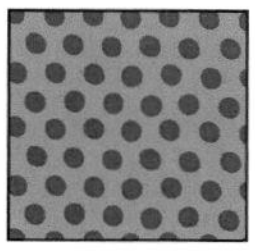

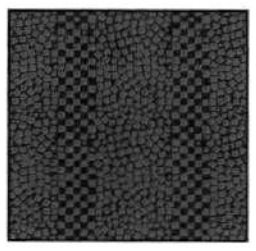

Backing and Binding Fabrics

Fabric 12
SEA URCHINS
Antique
PJ100AN

Fabric 5
SPOT
Magenta
GP70MG

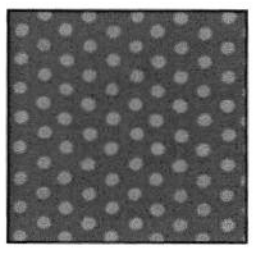

completing some rows. Sashing strips separate the blocks.

CUTTING OUT
Cut strips from the width of the fabric (unless otherwise instructed) and cross cut as described. As there are numerous pieces to cut for this quilt, cut from each fabric as shown below and then organize the pieces in groups for each block. (It is easier to construct each block if the component pieces are grouped together). The tables in the Making the Blocks section give the number and size of the pieces required for each block.

Fabric 2
For Blocks A, B and C cut 22 strips 1½in (3.8cm) wide and cross cut: 32 pieces 1½in x 12½in (3.8cm x 31.8cm); 32 pieces 1½in x 10½in (3.8cm x 26.7cm).

Fabric 3
For Block H cut 4 strips 2in (5.1cm) wide and cross cut: 8 pieces 2in x 9⅞in (5.1cm x 25.1cm); 8 pieces 2in x 6⅞in (5.1cm x 17.5cm).
For Blocks D and F cut 6 strips 2in (5.1cm) wide and cross cut: 12 pieces 2in x 9½in (5.1cm x 24.1cm); 12 pieces 2in x 6½in (5.1cm x 16.5cm).

For Block A cut 8 strips 1½in (3.8cm) wide and cross cut 2 of each of the following size pieces from each strip: 16 pieces 1½in x 10½in (3.8cm x 26.7in); 16 pieces 1½in x 8½in (3.8cm x 21.6cm).

Fabric 4

For Block C cut 4 strips 1½in (3.8cm) wide and cross cut: 8 pieces 1½in x 8½in (3.8cm x 21.6cm); 8 pieces 1½in x 6½in (3.8cm x 16.5cm).

Fabric 5

For Blocks A, B and C cut 10 strips 1½in (3.8cm) wide and cross cut: 32 pieces 1½in x 6½in (3.8cm x 16.5cm); 32 pieces 1½in x 4½in (3.8cm x 11.4cm).

Fabric 6

For Blocks A, B and C cut 2 strips 4½in (11.4cm) wide and cross cut: 16 squares 4½in x 4½in (11.4cm x 11.4cm).
For Block K cut 2 strips 2in (5.1cm) wide and cross cut: 2 pieces 2in x 13¼in (5.1cm x 33.7cm); 2 pieces 2in x 10¼in (5.1cm x 26cm).
For Block J cut 3 strips 2in (5.1cm) wide and cross cut: 4 pieces 2in x 12⅞in (5.1cm x 32.7cm); 4 pieces 2in x 9⅞in (5.1cm x 25.1cm).
For Blocks E, F and G cut 7 strips 2in (5.1cm) wide and cross cut: 10 pieces 2in x 12½in (5.1cm x 31.8cm); 10 pieces 2in x 9½in (5.1cm x 24.1cm).

Fabric 7

For Blocks A and B cut 10 strips 1½in (3.8cm) wide and cross cut: 24 pieces 1½in x 8½in (3.8cm x 21.6cm); 24 pieces 1½in x 6½in (3.8cm x 16.5cm).
For Blocks D, E, F and G cut 5 strips 2½in (6.4cm) wide and cross cut: 18 pieces 2½in x 6½in (6.4cm x 16.5cm); 18 squares 2½in x 2½in (6.4cm x 6.4cm).
For Blocks H and J cut 4 strips 2½in (6.4cm) wide and cross cut: 12 pieces 2½in x 6⅞in (6.4cm x 17.5cm); 12 pieces 2½in x 2⅞in (6.4cm x 7.3cm).
For Block K cut 1 strip 2½in (6.4cm) wide and cross cut: 2 pieces 2½in x 7¼in (6.4cm x 18.4cm); 2 pieces 2½in x 3¼in (6.4cm x 8.3cm).

Fabric 8

For Block K cut a piece 3¼in (8.3cm) from the end of the strip of fabric and trim it down to 1 square 3¼in x 3¼in (8.3cm x 8.3cm).
From the remaining fabric, for Blocks H and J cut 1 strip 2⅞in (7.3cm) wide and cross cut 6 squares 2⅞in x 2⅞in (7.3cm x 7.3cm).
From the remaining fabric, for Blocks D, E, F and G cut 1 strip 2½in (6.4cm) wide and cross cut 9 squares 2½in x 2½in (6.4cm x 6.4cm).

Fabric 9

For Block E cut 2 strips 2in (5.1cm) wide and cross cut: 4 pieces 2in x 9½in (5.1cm x 24.1cm); 4 pieces 2in x 6½in (5.1cm x 16.5cm).

Fabric 10

For Block K cut 1 strip 2in (5.1cm) wide and cross cut: 2 pieces 2in x 10¼in (5.1cm x 26cm); 2 pieces 2in x 7¼in (5.1cm x 18.4cm).
For Block J cut 2 strips 2in (5.1cm) wide and cross cut: 4 pieces 2in x 9⅞in (5.1cm x 25.1cm); 4 pieces 2in x 6⅞in (5.1cm x 17.5cm).
For Block G cut 1 strip 2in (5.1cm) wide and cross cut: 2 pieces 2in x 9½in (5.1cm x 24.1cm); 2 pieces 2in x 6½in (5.1cm x 16.5cm).
For Blocks B and C cut 8 strips 1½in (3.8cm) wide and cut 2 of each piece from each strip: 16 pieces 1½in x 10½in (3.8cm x 26.7cm); 16 pieces 1½in x 8½in (3.8cm x 21.6cm).

Fabric 11

For Block H cut 5 strips 2in (5.1cm) wide and cross cut: 8 pieces 2in x 12⅞in (5.1cm x 32.7cm); 8 pieces 2in x 9⅞in (5.1cm x 25.1cm).
For Block D cut 5 strips 2in (5.1cm) wide and cross cut: 8 pieces 2in x 12½in (5.1cm x 31.8cm); 8 pieces 2in x 9½in (5.1cm x 24.1cm).

LOG CABIN BLOCKS ASSEMBLY

Blocks A, B and C

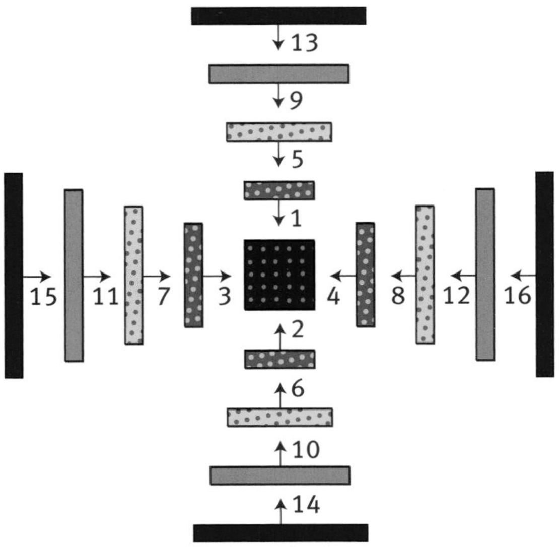

Blocks D, E, F, G, H, J and K

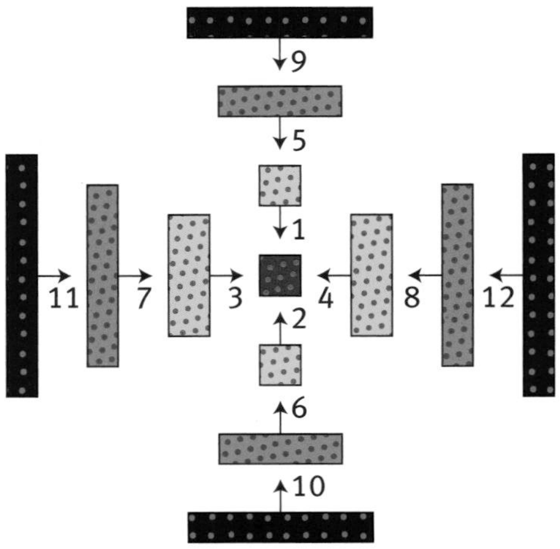

Sashing

From Fabric 1 cut 23 strips 2½in (6.4cm) wide. Cross cut 32 pieces 2½in x 12½in (6.4cm x 31.8cm). You can cut 3 pieces from each strip. From the remaining strips, cut and/or sew pieces the following sizes: 2 pieces 2½in x 100½in (6.4cm x 255.3cm); 2 pieces 2½in x 72½in (6.4cm x 184.2cm); 2 pieces 2½in x 44½in (6.4cm x 113cm); 2 pieces 2½in x 16½in (6.4cm x 41.9cm).

Backing

From Fabric 12 cut two pieces 40in x 87in (102cm x 221cm) and one piece 9in x 87in (22.8cm x 221cm).

Binding

From Fabric 5 cut 9 strips 2½in (6.4cm) wide. Remove selvedges and sew end to end.

MAKING THE BLOCKS

Use a ¼in (6mm) seam allowance throughout. The centre of the quilt is made up of 25 log cabin blocks (8 Block A, 4 Block B, 4 Block C, 4 Block D, 2 Block E, 2 Block F and 1 Block G). Follow the relevant Block Assembly Diagram and cut pieces as instructed in the relevant tables. Use a design wall to help place the patches in the correct design order.

Log Cabin Blocks A, B and C

The centre squares of these blocks are cut 4½in (11.4cm) square and are bordered by 4 rounds, each cut 1½in (3.8cm) wide. Completed blocks are 12½in (31.8cm) square. See Table 1 below.

Log Cabin Blocks D, E, F and G

The centre squares of these blocks are cut 2½in (6.4cm) square and are bordered by 3 rounds of strips. Completed blocks are 12½in (31.8cm) square. See Table 2 below.

TABLE 1 – LOG CABIN BLOCKS A, B AND C

	Width	Length	Block A Pieces	Block B Pieces	Block C Pieces
Centre	4½in (11.4cm)	4½in (11.4cm)	8 x Fabric 6	4 x Fabric 6	4 x Fabric 6
Round 1	1½in (3.8cm)	2 x 4½in (11.4cm) 2 x 6½in (16.5cm)	16 x Fabric 5 16 x Fabric 5	8 x Fabric 5 8 x Fabric 5	8 x Fabric 5 8 x Fabric 5
Round 2	1½in (3.8cm)	2 x 6½in (16.5cm) 2 x 8½in (21.6cm)	16 x Fabric 7 16 x Fabric 7	8 x Fabric 7 8 x Fabric 7	8 x Fabric 4 8 x Fabric 4
Round 3	1½in (3.8cm)	2 x 8½in (21.6cm) 2 x 10½in (26.7cm)	16 x Fabric 3 16 x Fabric 3	8 x Fabric 10 8 x Fabric 10	8 x Fabric 10 8 x Fabric 10
Round 4	1½in (3.8cm)	2 x 10½in (26.7cm) 2 x 12½in (31.8cm)	16 x Fabric 2 16 x Fabric 2	8 x Fabric 2 8 x Fabric 2	8 x Fabric 2 8 x Fabric 2

TABLE 2 – LOG CABIN BLOCKS D, E, F AND G

	Width	Length	Block D Pieces	Block E Pieces	Block F Pieces	Block G Pieces
Centre	2½in (6.4cm)	2½in (6.4cm)	4 x Fabric 8	2 x Fabric 8	2 x Fabric 8	1 x Fabric 8
Round 1	2½in (6.4cm)	2 x 2½in (6.4cm) 2 x 6½in (16.5cm)	8 x Fabric 7 8 x Fabric 7	4 x Fabric 7 4 x Fabric 7	4 x Fabric 7 4 x Fabric 7	2 x Fabric 7 2 x Fabric 7
Round 2	2in (5.1cm)	2 x 6½in (16.5cm) 2 x 9½in (24.1cm)	8 x Fabric 3 8 x Fabric 3	4 x Fabric 9 4 x Fabric 9	4 x Fabric 3 4 x Fabric 3	2 x Fabric 10 2 x Fabric 10
Round 3	2in (5.1cm)	2 x 9½in (24.1cm) 2 x 12½in (31.8cm)	8 x Fabric 11 8 x Fabric 11	4 x Fabric 6 4 x Fabric 6	4 x Fabric 6 4 x Fabric 6	2 x Fabric 6 2 x Fabric 6

TABLE 3 – SIDE SETTING TRIANGLES – BLOCKS H AND J

	Width	Length	Block H Pieces	Block J Pieces
Centre	2⅞in (7.3cm)	2⅞in (7.3cm)	4 x Fabric 8	2 x Fabric 8
Round 1	2½in (6.4cm)	2 x 2⅞in (7.3cm) 2 x 6⅞in (17.5cm)	8 x Fabric 7 8 x Fabric 7	4 x Fabric 7 4 x Fabric 7
Round 2	2in (5.1cm)	2 x 6⅞in (17.5cm) 2 x 9⅞in (25.1cm)	8 x Fabric 3 8 x Fabric 3	4 x Fabric 10 4 x Fabric 10
Round 3	2in (5.1cm)	2 x 9⅞in (25.1cm) 2 x 12⅞in (32.7cm)	8 x Fabric 11 8 x Fabric 11	4 x Fabric 6 4 x Fabric 6

TABLE 4 – CORNER TRIANGLES – BLOCK K

	Width	Length	Block K Pieces
Centre	3¼in (8.3cm)	3¼in (8.3cm)	1 x Fabric 8
Round 1	2½in (6.4cm)	2 x 3¼in (8.3cm) 2 x 7¼in (18.4cm)	2 x Fabric 7 2 x Fabric 7
Round 2	2in (5.1cm)	2 x 7¼in (18.4cm) 2 x 10¼in (26cm)	2 x Fabric 10 2 x Fabric 10
Round 3	2in (5.1cm)	2 x 10¼in (26cm) 2 x 13¼in (33.7cm)	2 x Fabric 6 2 x Fabric 6

Side Setting Triangles – Blocks H and J
Following the same principles make 12 half-square side blocks. These blocks are slightly larger than the main blocks. Completed blocks are 12⅞in (32.7cm) square. Diagonal seams are stay-stitched (see Note), then squares are cut once diagonally to form half-square triangle blocks. Make 4 Block H squares and 2 Block J squares to give 8 Block H setting triangles and 4 Block J setting triangles. See Table 3 above.

Corner Triangles – Block K
The 4 corner setting triangles are formed as 1 log cabin block, also slightly larger than the main blocks. The completed block is 13¼in (33.7cm) square. Both diagonal seams are stay-stitched (see Note), then the square is cut twice diagonally to form 4 quarter-square triangles. See Table 4 above.

Note for Blocks H, J and K This quilt is finished with setting triangles that leave bias edges on the outer edge of the quilt. Stabilize the quilt edges with stay stitching. Press each block.
For Blocks H and J draw a line diagonally from corner to corner. Stay stitch ⅜in (9mm) from each side of the line, then cut the block diagonally.
For Block K draw a line from corner to corner through both diagonals. Stay stitch ⅜in (9mm) from each side of both lines, then cut the block through both diagonals.

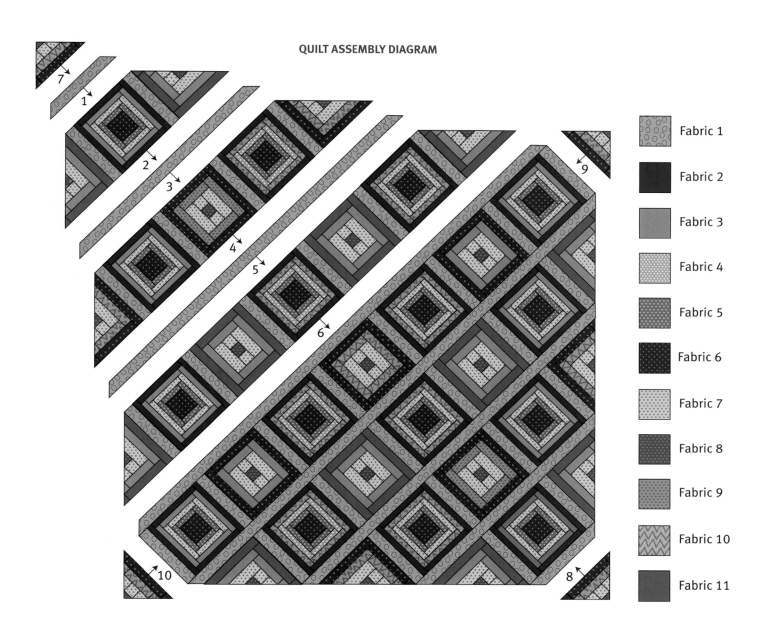

Fabric 1
Fabric 2
Fabric 3
Fabric 4
Fabric 5
Fabric 6
Fabric 7
Fabric 8
Fabric 9
Fabric 10
Fabric 11

BLOCK PLACEMENT DIAGRAM

MAKING THE QUILT

Lay out the blocks as shown in the Block Placement Diagram, adding the setting part-blocks and corner blocks. Add 2½in x 12½in (6.4cm x 31.8cm) sashing strips between each block to form diagonal rows, then add the long sashing strips between each row to complete the layout. Using a ¼in (6mm) seam allowance, sew the blocks, part-blocks and sashing strips together to form diagonal rows, following the Quilt Assembly Diagram. Pin the long sashing strips to the diagonal rows, first pinning the ends, then through the length, ensuring the strips do not stretch but lie flat against the blocks. Sew the sashing and rows together to complete the quilt top.

FINISHING THE QUILT

Sew the backing pieces together using a ¼in (6mm) seam allowance to form a piece approx. 87in x 87in (221cm x 221cm). Layer the quilt top, batting and backing, and baste together (see page 140).
Quilt as desired.
Trim the quilt edges and attach the binding (see page 141).

flaming hell *

Kaffe Fassett

When you have exciting, similarly toned (in this quilt, red) and large-scale prints to work with, *Flaming Hell* is the result. It is so simple to construct. Try any palette you fancy using this layout.

SIZE OF FINISHED QUILT
88in x 93in (224cm x 236cm)

FABRICS
Fabrics have been calculated at a maximum width of 40in (102cm), and are cut across the width, unless otherwise stated. Fabrics have been given a number – see Fabric Swatch Diagram for details.

Patchwork Fabrics
CHIPS
Fabric 1   Charcoal   ¼yd (25cm)
BALI BROCADE
Fabric 2   Red   ⅝yd (60cm)
SEA URCHINS
Fabric 3   Red   ¾yd (70cm)
TURKISH DELIGHT
Fabric 4   Red   2yd (1.9m)
(see note in Cutting Out)
Fabric 7   Wine   2½yd (2.3m)
LOTUS LEAF
Fabric 5   Wine   1⅜yd (1.3m)
LAKE BLOSSOMS
Fabric 6   Red   1½yd (1.4m)
ROSE AND HYDRANGEA
Fabric 8   Hot   ¾yd (70cm)

Backing and Binding Fabrics
FULL BLOWN
Fabric 9   Pink   3yd (2.8m)
* extra wide (108in/274cm)
SPOT
Fabric 10   Royal   ⅞yd (85cm)

Batting
96in x 101in (244cm x 257cm)

CUTTING OUT
Note: Only 1yd (90cm) of Fabric 4 is required if not fussy cutting and joining. Fabric is cut across the width unless otherwise stated. When the border strips are longer than 40in (102cm) – the width of the fabric – join strips end to end to obtain the required length. Use a ¼in (6mm) seam allowance and press seams open.

Centre Panel
From Fabric 8 cut a rectangle 12½in x 17½in (31.8cm x 44.5cm). A generous amount of fabric has been allowed so the centre panel can be cut to best effect.

Border 1
From Fabric 1 cut 2 strips 2½in (6.4cm) wide and cut borders as follows:
2 borders 2½in x 17½in (6.4cm x 44.5cm) for the sides;
2 borders 2½in x 16½in (6.4cm x 41.9cm) for the top and bottom.

Border 2
From Fabric 2 cut 4 strips 6½in (16.5cm) wide and cut borders as follows:
2 borders 6½in x 21½in (16.5cm x 54.6cm) for the sides;
2 borders 6½in x 28½in (16.5cm x 72.4cm) for the top and bottom.

Border 3
From Fabric 3 cut 4 strips 6½in (16.5cm) wide and cut/sew borders as follows:
2 borders 6½in x 33½in (16.5cm x 85.1cm) for the sides;
2 borders 6½in x 40½in (16.5cm x 103cm) for the top and bottom.

Border 4
From Fabric 4 cut 4 pairs of identical strips 6½in (16.5cm) wide, centring the motifs in the strip and carefully joining 2 strips together to create the required length of motifs. Extra fabric has been included as required. Cut/sew borders as follows:
2 borders 6½in x 45½in (16.5cm x 115.6cm) for the sides;
2 borders 6½in x 52½in (16.5cm x 133.4cm) for the top and bottom.

Border 5
From Fabric 5 cut 7 strips 6½in (16.5cm) wide and cross cut/sew borders as follows:
2 borders 6½in x 57½in (16.5cm x 146.1cm) for the sides;
2 borders 6½in x 64½in (16.5cm x 163.8cm) for the top and bottom.

FABRIC SWATCH DIAGRAM

Patchwork Fabrics

Fabric 1
CHIPS
Charcoal
BM73CC

Fabric 2
BALI BROCADE
Red
BM69RD

Fabric 3
SEA URCHINS
Red
PJ100RD

Fabric 4
TURKISH DELIGHT
Red
GP81RD

Fabric 5
LOTUS LEAF
Wine
GP29WN

Fabric 6
LAKE BLOSSOMS
Red
GP93RD

Fabric 7
TURKISH DELIGHT
Wine
GP81WN

Fabric 8
ROSE AND HYDRANGEA
Hot
PJ97HT

Backing and Binding Fabrics

Fabric 9
FULL BLOWN
Pink
QB04PK

Fabric 10
SPOT
Royal
GP70RY

Border 6
From Fabric 6 cut 8 strips 6½in (16.5cm) wide and cross cut/sew borders as follows:
2 borders 6½in x 69½in (16.5cm x 176.5cm) for the sides;
2 borders 6½in x 76½in (16.5cm x 194.3cm) for the top and bottom.

Border 7
From Fabric 7 cut 4 strips 6½in (16.5cm) **down the length of the fabric** centring motifs along the middle of the strips.
Trim as follows:
2 borders 6½in x 81½in (16.5cm x 207cm) for the sides;
2 borders 6½in x 88½in (16.5cm x 224.8cm) for the top and bottom.

Backing
From Fabric 9 cut 1 piece approx. 96in x 101in (244cm x 257cm).

Binding
From Fabric 10 cut 11 strips 2½in (6.4cm) wide and sew end to end (see page 141).

MAKING THE QUILT
Use a ¼in (6mm) seam allowance throughout. Refer to the Quilt Assembly Diagram and, starting with Border 1, sew the strips to the centre panel, adding the side strips first and then top and bottom strips. To avoid the long borders stretching, pin each border in place before sewing. Press each border seam as you add it. Continue in this way, following the number order on the diagram, until all 7 borders have been added to the quilt.

FINISHING THE QUILT
Press the quilt top. Layer the quilt top, batting and backing, and baste together (see page 140).
Quilt as desired.
Trim the quilt edges and attach the binding (see page 141).

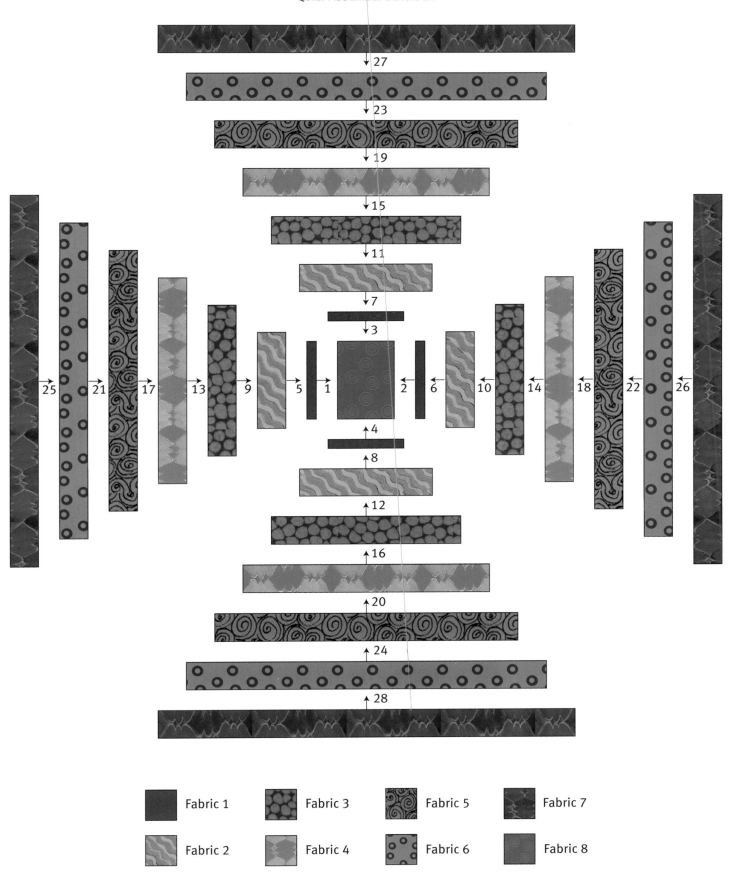

Fabric 1

Fabric 2

Fabric 3

Fabric 4

Fabric 5

Fabric 6

Fabric 7

Fabric 8

hot steps *

Kaffe Fassett

Most of the prints in this playful quilt feature round motifs – it's like a juggling act in a circus. This is such a simple layout but so full of movement, ideal for anyone wanting to make a quilt for the first time.

SIZE OF FINISHED QUILT
77½in x 94in (197 cm x 239cm)

FABRICS
Fabrics have been calculated at a maximum width of 40in (102cm), and are cut across the width, unless otherwise stated. Fabrics have been given a number – see Fabric Swatch Diagram for details.

Patchwork Fabrics
JUMBLE
Fabric 1	Scarlet	⅝yd (60cm)
Fabric 2	Black	⅜yd (40cm)

ORANGES
Fabric 3	Lime	⅝yd (60cm)
Fabric 4	Orange	⅝yd (60cm)
Fabric 5	Yellow	⅝yd (60cm)
Fabric 6	Red	⅜yd (40cm)

*see also Backing Fabric
GEODES
Fabric 7	Black	¼yd (25cm)
Fabric 8	Red	⅜yd (40cm)

OMBRE LEAVES
Fabric 9	Pink	⅜yd (40cm)
Fabric 10	Green	⅜yd (40cm)
Fabric 11	Orange	⅝yd (60cm)

BUSY LIZZY
Fabric 12	Red	¼yd (25cm)
Fabric 13	Black	½yd (45cm)

PRIMULAS
Fabric 14	Blue	⅜yd (40cm)

MOSAIC CIRCLES
Fabric 15	Black	⅜yd (40cm)
Fabric 16	Red	⅜yd (40cm)

PROMENADE STRIPE
Fabric 17	Hot	2⅜yd (2.25m)

TURKISH DELIGHT
Fabric 18	Wine	¼yd (25cm)

* must include row of whole motifs

Backing and Binding Fabrics
ORANGES
Fabric 6	Red	7¼yd (6.7m)

* see also Patchwork Fabrics
MAD PLAID
Fabric 19	Maroon	¾yd (70cm)

FABRIC SWATCH DIAGRAM

Patchwork Fabrics

Fabric 1
JUMBLE
Scarlet
BM53SC

Fabric 2
JUMBLE
Black
BM53BK

Fabric 3
ORANGES
Lime
GP177LM

Fabric 4
ORANGES
Orange
GP177OR

Fabric 5
ORANGES
Yellow
GP177YE

Fabric 6
ORANGES
Red
GP177RD

Fabric 7
GEODES
Black
PJ99BK

Fabric 8
GEODES
Red
PJ99RD

Fabric 9
OMBRE LEAVES
Pink
GP174PK

Fabric 10
OMBRE LEAVES
Green
GP174GN

Fabric 11
OMBRE LEAVES
Orange
GP174OR

Fabric 12
BUSY LIZZY
Red
GP175RD

Fabric 13
BUSY LIZZY
Black
GP175BK

Fabric 14
PRIMULAS
Blue
BM71BL

Fabric 15
MOSAIC CIRCLES
Black
GP176BK

Fabric 16
MOSAIC CIRCLES
Red
GP176RD

Fabric 17
PROMENADE STRIPE
Hot
GP178HT

Fabric 18
TURKISH DELIGHT
Wine
GP81WN

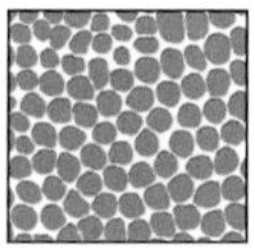

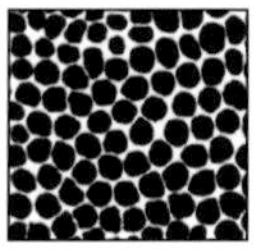

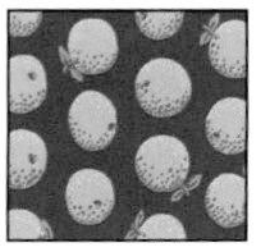

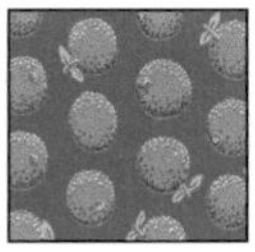

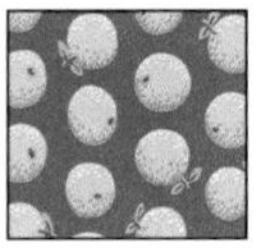

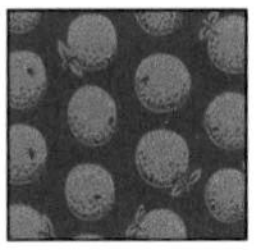

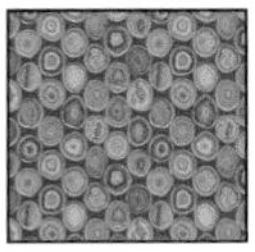

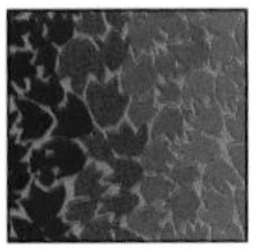

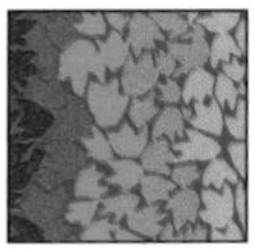

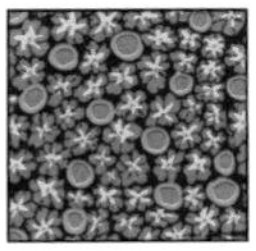

Backing and Binding Fabrics

Fabric 6
ORANGES
Red
GP177RD

Fabric 19
MAD PLAID
Maroon
BM37MR

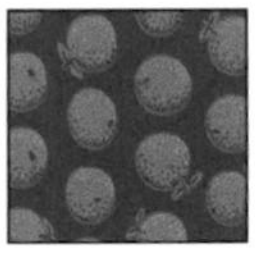

Batting
86in x 102in (218cm x 259cm)

PATCH SHAPES
Patches are 5½in (14cm) squares (finished), cut from strips and cross cut into squares. The squares are straight set in 15 rows of 12. Use a design wall to help place the patches in the correct design order.

CUTTING OUT
Cut strips from the width of the fabric and cross cut as described.

Squares
Cut strips 6in (15.2cm) wide and cross cut squares 6in (15.2cm). Each strip will give you 6 squares.
Cut a total of 180 squares from fabrics as follows:
Fabric 1 (3 strips) 13 squares;
Fabric 2 (2 strips) 12 squares;
Fabric 3 (3 strips)13 squares;
Fabric 4 (3 strips) 18 squares;
Fabric 5 (3 strips) 18 squares;
Fabric 6 (2 strips) 8 squares;
Fabric 7 (1 strip) 5 squares;
Fabric 8 (2 strips) 10 squares;
Fabric 9 (2 strips) 11 squares;
Fabric 10 (2 strips) 7 squares;
Fabric 11 (3 strips) 13 squares;
Fabric 12 (1 strip) 6 squares;
Fabric 13 (3 strips) 15 squares;
Fabric 14 (2 strips) 11 squares;
Fabric 15 (2 strips) 9 squares;
Fabric 16 (2 strips) 11 squares.

Border and Corner Squares
Border: from Fabric 17 cut down the length of the fabric 2 strips 6in x 83in (15.2cm x 210.8cm) and 2 strips 6in x 66½in (15.2cm x 168.9cm).
For the corner squares, from Fabric 18, fussy cut 4 different motifs into squares 6in x 6in (15.2cm x 15.2cm).

Backing
From Fabric 6 cut 2 pieces 40in x 86in (102cm x 218cm) and 1 piece 23in x 86in (58cm x 218cm). Sew the 3 pieces together to form a piece approx 86in x 102in (218cm x 259cm).

Binding
From Fabric 19 cut 9 strips 2½in (6.4cm) wide across the width of the fabric and sew end to end (see page 141).

MAKING THE QUILT
Use a ¼in (6mm) seam allowance throughout. Arrange the squares following the Quilt Assembly Diagram. Lay out the squares in 15 rows of 12 to form the centre of the quilt. Sew the squares together 1 row at a time, pressing seams in opposite directions on alternate rows – odd rows to the left, even rows to the right – this will allow the finished seams to sit flat. Sew the 15 rows together, carefully matching seams.

Borders and Corner Squares
Sew the 2 long border strips to each side of the quilt centre. Sew a corner square to each end of the 2 short borders. Pin and sew these 2 borders to the top and bottom of the quilt.

FINISHING THE QUILT
Press the quilt top. Layer the quilt top, batting and backing, and baste together (see page 140).
Quilt as desired.
Trim the quilt edges and attach the binding (see page 141).

QUILT ASSEMBLY DIAGRAM

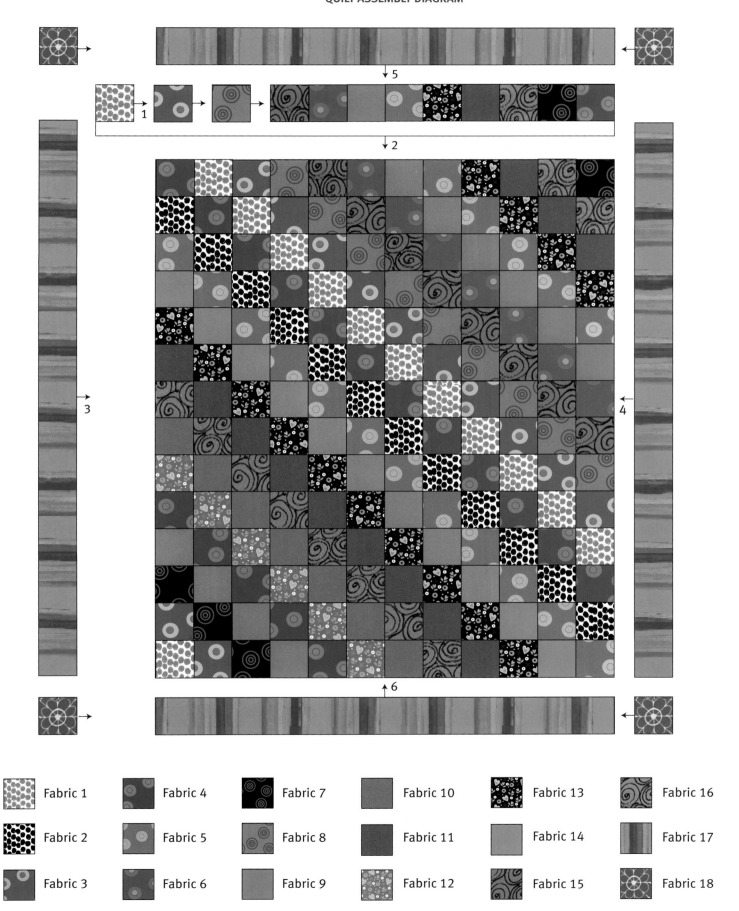

Fabric 1	Fabric 4	Fabric 7	Fabric 10	Fabric 13	Fabric 16
Fabric 2	Fabric 5	Fabric 8	Fabric 11	Fabric 14	Fabric 17
Fabric 3	Fabric 6	Fabric 9	Fabric 12	Fabric 15	Fabric 18

cool steps *

Kaffe Fassett

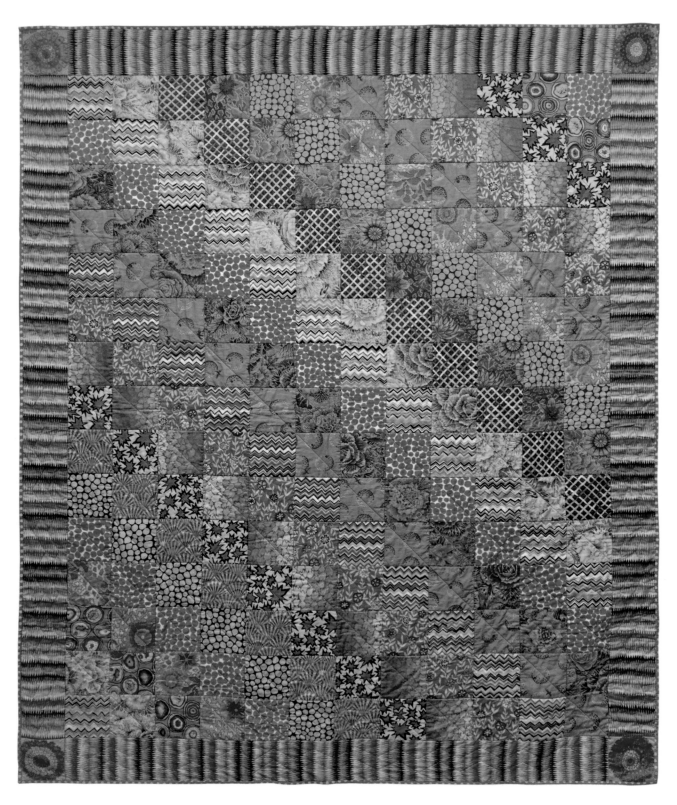

A cool version of Hot Steps shows how any layout in this book can be made in your own personal colour scheme. It's intriguing how different this quilt looks with its frosty palette.

SIZE OF FINISHED QUILT
77½in x 94in (197 cm x 239cm)

FABRICS
Fabrics have been calculated at a maximum width of 40in (102cm), and are cut across the width, unless otherwise stated. Fabrics have been given a number – see Fabric Swatch Diagram for details.

Patchwork Fabrics
JUMBLE
Fabric 1	Cobalt	⅝yd (60cm)
Fabric 2	Duck Egg	⅜yd (40cm)
Fabric 3	Rose	¼yd (25cm)

BANG
Fabric 4	Contrast	⅜yd (40cm)

OMBRE LEAVES
Fabric 5	Grey	⅝yd (60cm)

BUSY LIZZY
Fabric 6	Blue	⅝yd (60cm)

ORANGES
Fabric 7	Blue	⅝yd (60cm)

DREAM
Fabric 8	Aqua	⅜yd (40cm)
Fabric 9	Blue	⅜yd (40cm)

MAD PLAID
Fabric 10	Contrast	⅜yd (40cm)

BRASSICA
Fabric 11	Green	⅝yd (60cm)
Fabric 12	Blue	⅜yd (40cm)

ZIG ZAG
Fabric 13	Sky	⅜yd (40cm)
Fabric 14	Contrast	⅝yd (60cm)

PAPER FANS
Fabric 15	Cool	⅜yd (40cm)

GEODES
Fabric 16	Grey	¼yd (25cm)

DIAMOND STRIPE
Fabric 17	Blue	2½yd (2.3m)

TURKISH DELIGHT
Fabric 18	Aqua	½yd (45cm)
*must include row of whole motifs

Backing and Binding Fabrics
FULL BLOWN
Fabric 19	Blue	3yd (2.8m)
* extra wide fabric 108in (274cm)

SPOT
Fabric 20	Storm	¾yd (70cm)

FABRIC SWATCH DIAGRAM

Patchwork Fabrics

Fabric 1
JUMBLE
Cobalt
BM53CB

Fabric 2
JUMBLE
Duck Egg
BM53DE

Fabric 3
JUMBLE
Rose
BM53RO

Fabric 4
BANG
Contrast
BM72CN

Fabric 5
OMBRE LEAVES
Grey
GP174GY

Fabric 6
BUSY LIZZY
Blue
GP175BL

Fabric 7
ORANGES
Blue
GP177BL

Fabric 8
DREAM
Aqua
GP148AQ

Fabric 9
DREAM
Blue
GP148BL

Fabric 10
MAD PLAID
Contrast
BM37CN

Fabric 11
BRASSICA
Green
PJ51GN

Fabric 12
BRASSICA
Blue
PJ51BL

Fabric 13
ZIG ZAG
Sky
BM43SK

Fabric 14
ZIG ZAG
Contrast
BM43CN

Fabric 15
PAPER FANS
Cool
GP143CL

Fabric 16
GEODES
Grey
PJ99GY

Fabric 17
DIAMOND STRIPE
Blue
GP170BL

Fabric 18
TURKISH DELIGHT
Aqua
GP81AQ

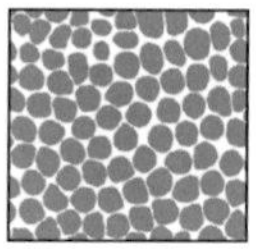

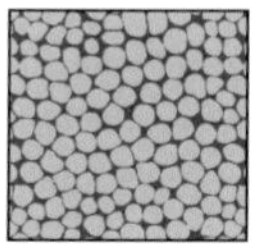

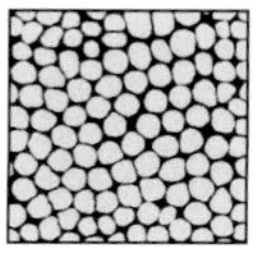

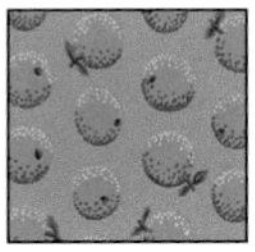

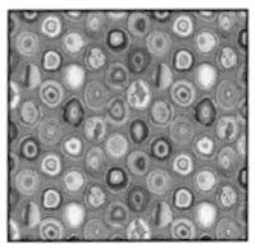

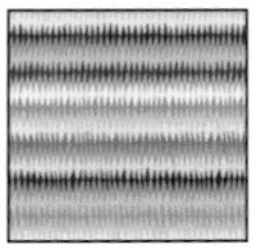

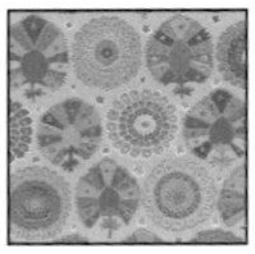

Backing and Binding Fabrics

Fabric 19
FULL BLOWN
Blue
QB04BL

Fabric 20
SPOT
Storm
GP70SR

Batting
86in x 102in (218cm x 259cm)

PATCH SHAPES

Patches are 5½in (14cm) squares (finished), cut from strips and cross cut into squares. The squares are straight set in 15 rows of 12. Use a design wall to help place the patches in the correct design order.

CUTTING OUT

Cut strips from the width of the fabric and cross cut as described.

Squares

Cut strips 6in (15.2cm) wide and cross cut squares 6in (15.2cm). Each strip will give you 6 squares.
Cut a total of 180 squares from fabrics as follows:
Fabric 1 (3 strips) 18 squares;
Fabric 2 (2 strips) 8 squares;
Fabric 3 (1 strip) 6 squares;
Fabric 4 (2 strips) 11 squares;
Fabric 5 (3 strips) 13 squares;
Fabric 6 (3 strips) 15 squares;
Fabric 7 (3 strips) 18 squares;
Fabric 8 2 (strips) 11 squares;
Fabric 9 (2 strips) 9 squares;
Fabric 10 (2 strips) 10 squares;
Fabric 11 (3 strips) 13 squares;
Fabric 12 (2 strips) 12 squares;
Fabric 13 (2 strips) 11 squares;
Fabric 14 (3 strips) 13 squares;
Fabric 15 (2 strips) 7 squares;
Fabric 16 (1 strip) 5 squares

Border and Corner Squares

For the border: from Fabric 17 cut down the length of the fabric 2 strips 6in x 83in (15.2cm x 210.8cm) and cut 2 strips 6in x 66½in (15.2cm x 168.9cm).
For the corner squares: from Fabric 18 fussy cut 4 different motifs into squares 6in x 6in (15.2cm x 15.2cm).

Backing

From Fabric 19 cut a piece 86in x 102in (218cm x 259cm).

Binding

From Fabric 20 cut 9 strips 2½in (6.4cm) wide across the width of the fabric and sew end to end (see page 141).

MAKING THE QUILT

Use a ¼in (6mm) seam allowance throughout. Arrange the squares following the Quilt Assembly Diagram opposite. Following the procedure shown in the Quilt Assembly Diagram for Hot Steps on page 109, lay out the squares in 15 rows of 12 to form the centre of the quilt. Sew the squares together 1 row at a time, pressing seams in opposite directions on alternate rows – odd rows to the left, even rows to the right – as this will allow the finished seams to sit flat. Sew the 15 rows together, carefully matching seams.

Borders and Corner Squares

Sew the 2 long border strips to each side of the quilt centre. Sew a corner square to each end of the 2 short borders. Pin and sew them to the top and bottom of the quilt.

FINISHING THE QUILT

Press the quilt top. Layer the quilt top, batting and backing, and baste together (see page 140).
Quilt as desired.
Trim the quilt edges and attach the binding (see page 141).

QUILT ASSEMBLY DIAGRAM

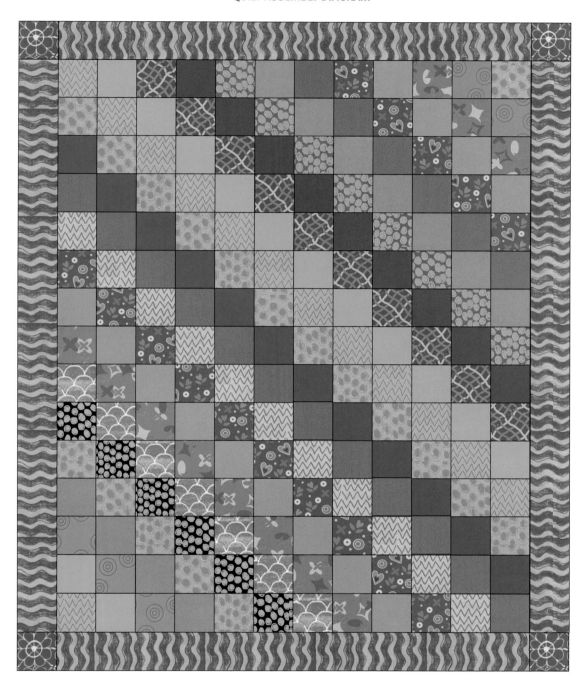

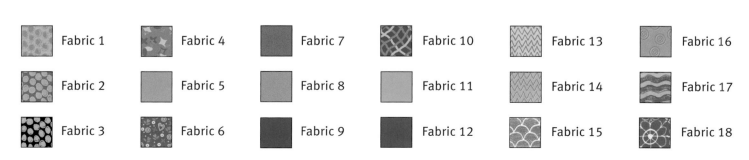

	Fabric 1		Fabric 4		Fabric 7		Fabric 10		Fabric 13		Fabric 16
	Fabric 2		Fabric 5		Fabric 8		Fabric 11		Fabric 14		Fabric 17
	Fabric 3		Fabric 6		Fabric 9		Fabric 12		Fabric 15		Fabric 18

green with envy *

Brandon Mably

This cool green version of *Flaming Hell* had Brandon playing with such a different take on my quilt.

SIZE OF FINISHED QUILT
88in x 93in (224cm x 236cm)

FABRICS
Fabrics have been calculated at a maximum width of 40in (102cm), and are cut across the width, unless otherwise stated. Fabrics have been given a number – see Fabric Swatch Diagram for details.

Patchwork Fabrics
ORANGES
Fabric 1	Red	¼yd (25cm)
Fabric 7	Lime	2yd (1.9m)

BALI BROCADE
Fabric 2	Purple	¾yd (70cm)

JAPANESE CHRYSANTHEMUM
Fabric 3	Green	¾yd (70cm)

PROMENADE STRIPE
Fabric 4	Cold	1½yd (1.4m)

LOTUS LEAF
Fabric 5	Purple	1⅜yd (1.3m)

* see also Binding Fabric

CHIPS
Fabric 6	Blue	1½yd (1.4m)

TURKISH DELIGHT
Fabric 8	Black	¾yd (70cm)

Backing and Binding Fabrics
FULL BLOWN
Fabric 9	Blue	3yd (2.8m)

* extra wide (108in/274cm)

LOTUS LEAF
Fabric 5	Purple	¾yd (70cm)

* see also Patchwork Fabrics

Batting
96in x 101in (244cm x 257cm)

CUTTING OUT
When the border strips are longer than 40in (102cm) – the usable width of the fabric – join strips end to end to obtain the required length. Use a ¼in (6mm) seam and press seams open.

Centre Panel
From Fabric 8 cut a rectangle 12½in x 17½in (31.8cm x 44.5cm).
Note: a generous amount of fabric has been allowed so the centre panel can be cut to best effect.

Border 1
From Fabric 1 fussy cut 2 strips 2½in (6.4cm) wide, centring the oranges along the strip, and cut borders as follows: 2 borders 2½in x 17½in (6.4cm x 44.5cm) for the sides; 2 borders 2½in x 16½in (6.4cm x 41.9cm) for the top and bottom.

Border 2
From Fabric 2 cut 4 strips 6½in (16.5cm) wide and cut borders as follows: 2 borders 6½in x 21½in (16.5cm x 54.6cm) for the sides; 2 borders 6½in x 28½in (16.5cm x 72.4cm) for the top and bottom.

Border 3
From Fabric 3 cut 4 strips 6½in (16.5cm) wide and cut borders as follows: 2 borders 6½in x 33½in (16.5cm x 85.1cm) for the sides; 2 borders 6½in x 40½in (16.5cm x 103cm) for the top and bottom.

Border 4
From Fabric 4 cut 4 strips 6½in (16.5cm) wide down the length of the fabric, parallel with the selvedges, as follows: 2 strips 6½in x 45½in (16.5cm x 115.6cm) for the sides; 2 strips 6½in x 52½in (16.5cm x 133.4cm) for the top and bottom.

Border 5
From Fabric 5 cut 7 strips 6½in (16.5cm) wide and cross cut/sew borders as follows: 2 strips 6½in x 57½in (16.5cm x 146.1cm) for the sides;2 strips 6½in x 64½in (16.5cm x 164cm) for the top and bottom.

Border 6
From Fabric 6 cut 8 strips 6½in (16.5cm) wide and cross cut/sew borders as follows: 2 strips 6½in x 69½in (16.5cm x 176.5cm) for the sides;2 strips 6½in x 76½in (16.5cm x 194.3cm) for the top and bottom.

Border 7
From Fabric 7 cut 10 strips 6½in (16.5cm) wide and cross cut/sew borders as follows: 2 strips 6½in x 81½in (16.5cm x 207cm) for the sides; 2 strips 6½in x 88½in (16.5cm x 224.8cm) for the top and bottom.
Note: extra fabric has been allowed to enable fussy cutting strips to centralise the orange motifs both along the borders and across the borders.

FABRIC SWATCH DIAGRAM

Patchwork Fabrics

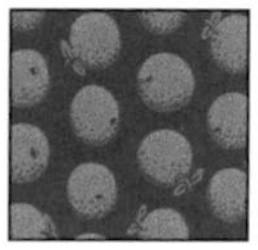

Fabric 1
ORANGES
Red
GP177RD

Fabric 2
BALI BROCADE
Purple
BM69PU

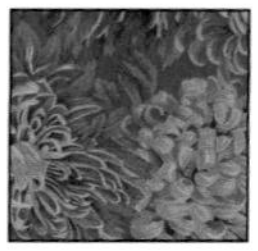

Fabric 3
JAPANESE CHRYSANTHEMUM
Green
PJ41GN

Fabric 4
PROMENADE STRIPE
Cold
GP178CD

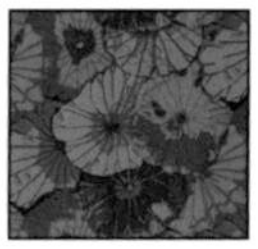

Fabric 5
LOTUS LEAF
Purple
GP29PU

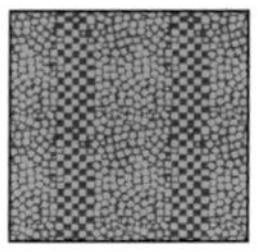

Fabric 6
CHIPS
Blue
BM73BL

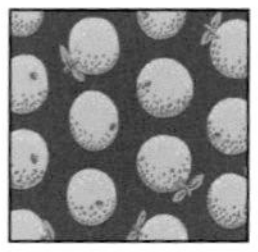

Fabric 7
ORANGES
Lime
GP177LM

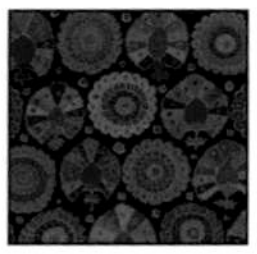

Fabric 8
TURKISH DELIGHT
Black
GP81BK

Backing and Binding Fabrics

Fabric 9
FULL BLOWN
Blue
QB04BL

Fabric 5
LOTUS LEAF
Purple
GP29PU

Backing
From Fabric 9 cut 1 piece approx. 96in x 101in (244cm x 257cm).

Binding
From Fabric 5 cut 10 strips 2½in (6.4cm) wide. Remove selvedges and sew end to end.

MAKING THE QUILT
Use ¼in (6mm) seams throughout. Refer to the Quilt Assembly Diagram and, starting with Border 1, sew the strips to the centre panel, adding the side strips first and then top and bottom strips. To avoid the long borders stretching, pin each border in place before sewing. Press each border as you add it. Continue in this way, following the number order on the diagram, until all 7 borders have been added to the quilt.

FINISHING THE QUILT
Press the quilt top. Layer the quilt top, batting and backing, and baste together (see page 140).
Quilt as desired.
Trim the quilt edges and attach the binding (see page 141).

QUILT ASSEMBLY DIAGRAM

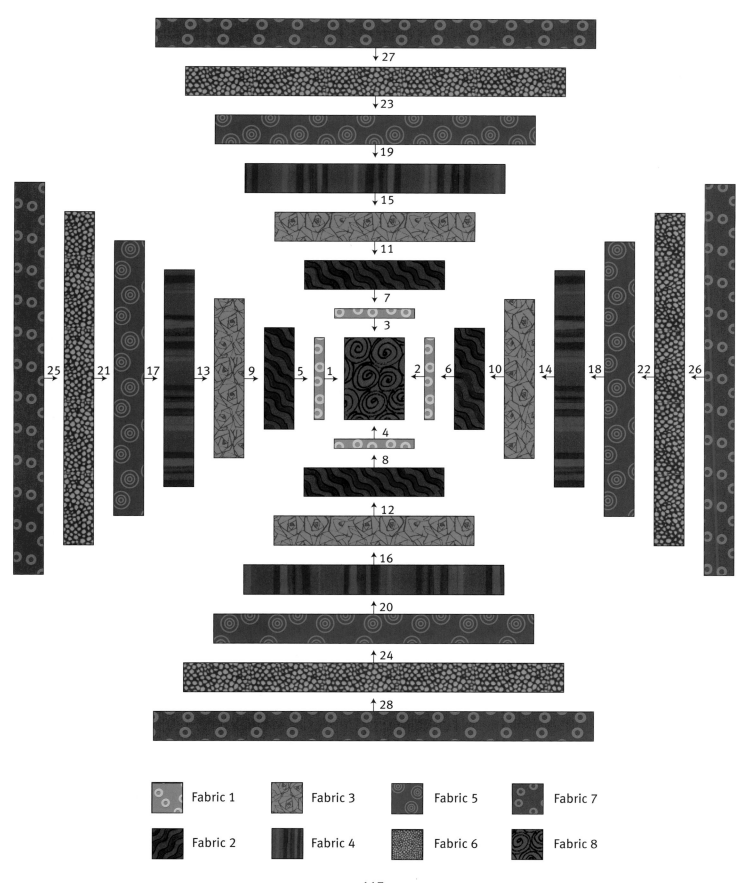

Fabric 1

Fabric 3

Fabric 5

Fabric 7

Fabric 2

Fabric 4

Fabric 6

Fabric 8

framed log cabin *

Kaffe Fassett

I liked the idea of a huge-scale log cabin. Frames using rosy tones in small-scale prints around each 'log' show off the large-scale prints to great effect.

SIZE OF FINISHED QUILT
86½in x 86½in (220cm x 220cm)

FABRICS
Fabrics have been calculated at a maximum width of 40in (102cm), and are cut across the width, unless otherwise stated. Fabrics have been given a number – see Fabric Swatch Diagram for details.

Patchwork Fabrics
BANG
| Fabric 1 | Yellow | ¼yd (25cm) |

GEODES
| Fabric 2 | Gold | ½yd (45cm) |

ROSE AND HYDRANGEA
| Fabric 3 | Citrus | ¾yd (70cm) |

CACTUS FLOWER
| Fabric 4 | Yellow | 1⅞yd (1.8m) |

* cut down fabric length or
* cut across fabric width 1¼yd (1.2m)

BALI BROCADE
| Fabric 5 | Yellow | 2yd (1.9m) |

SPOT
Fabric 6	Fuchsia	¾yd (70cm)
Fabric 7	Melon	¼yd (25cm)
Fabric 8	Orange	⅝yd (60cm)
Fabric 9	Shocking	⅜yd (40cm)

ABORIGINAL DOT
Fabric 10	Cantaloupe	⅜yd (40cm)
Fabric 11	Orange	¼yd (25cm)
Fabric 12	Shocking	½yd (45cm)

ONION RINGS
| Fabric 13 | Cocoa | ⅝yd (60cm) |

Backing and Binding Fabrics
FULL BLOWN
| Fabric 14 | Pink | 2¾yd (2.6m) |

* extra-wide fabric 108in (274cm)

MILLEFIORE
| Fabric 15 | Green | ¾yd (70cm) |

Batting
95in x 95in (241cm x 241cm)

PATCH SHAPES
Each 'log' has a feature fabric surrounded by a small-scale print 'frame'.

FABRIC SWATCH DIAGRAM

Patchwork Fabrics

Fabric 1
BANG
Yellow
BM72YE

Fabric 2
GEODES
Gold
PJ99GD

Fabric 3
ROSE AND HYDRANGEA
Citrus
PJ97CT

Fabric 4
CACTUS FLOWER
Yellow
PJ96YE

Fabric 5
BALI BROCADE
Yellow
BM69YE

Fabric 6
SPOT
Fuchsia
GP70FU

Fabric 7
SPOT
Melon
GP70ME

Fabric 8
SPOT
Orange
GP70OR

Fabric 9
SPOT
Shocking
GP70SG

Fabric 10
ABORIGINAL DOT
Cantaloupe
GP71CA

Fabric 11
ABORIGINAL DOT
Orange
GP71OR

Fabric 12
ABORIGINAL DOT
Shocking
GP71SG

Fabric 13
ONION RINGS
Cocoa
BM70CO

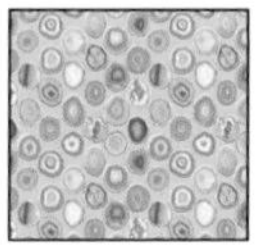

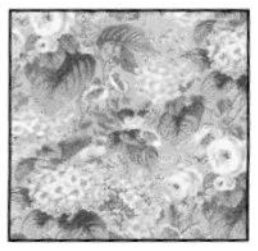

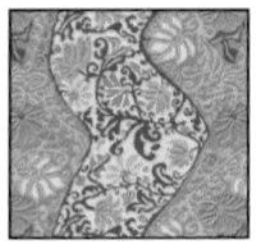

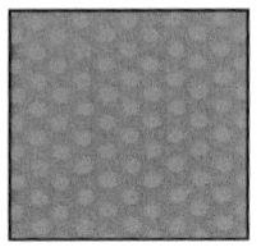

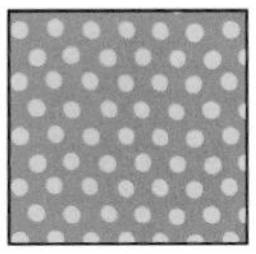

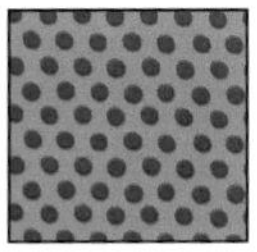

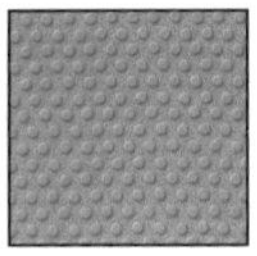

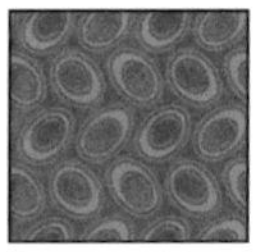

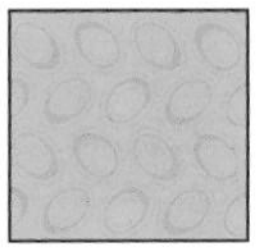

Backing and Binding Fabrics

Fabric 14
FULL BLOWN
Pink
QB04PK

Fabric 15
MILLEFIORE
Green
GP92GN

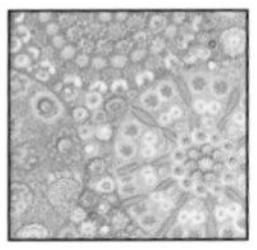

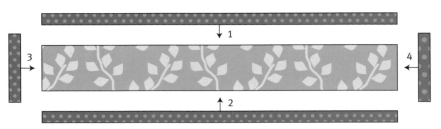

CUTTING OUT

Unless otherwise stated, fabrics are cut across the width of the fabric.

Feature Fabrics for Logs

Cut strips as follows:
Fabric 1: 2 strips 3½in (8.9cm) wide;
Fabric 2: 3 strips 4½in (11.4cm) wide;
Fabric 3: 4 strips 5½in (14cm) wide;
Fabric 4: 4 strips (down the length of the fabric) 6½in (16.5cm) wide;
Fabric 5: 9 strips 7½in (19.1cm) wide.

Small-scale Fabrics for Frames

Cut strips 2in (5.1cm) wide from the following fabrics:
Fabric 6: 11 strips;
Fabric 7: 3 strips;
Fabric 8: 9 strips;
Fabric 9: 5 strips;
Fabric 10: 5 strips;
Fabric 11: 3 strips;
Fabric 12: 6 strips;
Fabric 13: 10 strips.

There are 5 rounds of framed logs around a central framed square. Logs have been given letters to indicate the order sewn, as shown in the Cutting Table and Quilt Assembly Diagram. Refer to the Cutting Table for Log and Frame cutting measurements. Strips will need to be sewn together (selvedges removed) to make the required length for many of the logs and frames.

Backing

Trim Fabric 14 to 95in (241cm) square.

Binding

From Fabric 15 cut 9 strips 2½in (6.4cm) wide and sew end to end (see page 141).

MAKING THE QUILT

Assembling the logs

Follow the Cutting Table for required log and frame sizes. Use a ¼in (6mm) seam allowance throughout. For each log, sew the longer top and bottom frames to the log first, then the shorter side frames. Refer to the Block Assembly Diagram.

Assembling the top

Lay out the quilt on a design wall and check each log is in the correct position. Following the Quilt Assembly Diagram (see page 122), start with the centre square A and work in the sequence of the log letters: sew B to A, then C to AB, then D to ABC, then E to ABCD and so on. It is best to pin each piece before sewing, especially for the longer logs.

FINISHING THE QUILT

Press the quilt top. Layer the quilt top, batting and backing, and baste together (see page 140).
Quilt as desired.
Trim the quilt edges and attach the binding (see page 141).

	Log Fabric No.	Log Size	Frame Fabric No.	Frame Top and Bottom (long sides) All 2in (5.1cm) wide	Frame Sides (short sides) All 2in (5.1cm) wide
Centre and Round 1 (anti-clockwise)			**Completed size: 18½in (47cm) square**		
A	1	3½in x 3½in (8.9cm x 8.9cm)	9	2 x 3½in (8.9cm)	2 x 6½in (16.5cm)
B	1	3½in x 3½in (8.9cm x 8.9cm)	11	2 x 3½in (8.9cm)	2 x 6½in (16.5cm)
C	1	3½in x 9½in (8.9cm x 24.1cm)	10	2 x 9½in (24.1cm)	2 x 6½in (16.5cm)
D	1	3½in x 9½in (8.9cm x 24.1cm)	7	2 x 9½in (24.1cm)	2 x 6½in (16.5cm)
E	1	3½in x 15½in (8.9cm x 39.4cm)	10	2 x 15½in (39.4cm)	2 x 6½in (16.5cm)
Round 2 (anti-clockwise)			**Completed size: 32½in (82.6cm) square**		
F	2	4½in x 15½in (11.4cm x 39.4 cm)	12	2 x 15½in (39.4cm)	2 x 7½in (19.1cm)
G	2	4½in x 22½in (11.4cm x 55.9cm)	13	2 x 22½ in (55.9cm)	2 x 7½in (19.1cm)
H	2	4½in x 22½in (11.4cm x 55.9cm)	12	2 x 22½in (55.9cm)	2 x 7½in (19.1cm)
I	2	4½in x 29½in (11.4cm x 74.9cm)	7	2 x 29½in (74.9cm)	2 x 7½in (19.1cm)
Round 3 (clockwise)			**Completed size: 48½in (123.2cm) square**		
J	3	5½in x 29½in (14cm x 74.9cm)	8	2 x 29½in (74.9cm)	2 x 8½in (21.6cm)
K	3	5½in x 37½in (14cm x 95.3cm)	11	2 x 37½in (95.3cm)	2 x 8½in (21.6cm)
L	3	5½in x 37½in (14cm x 95.3cm)	8	2 x 37½in (95.3cm)	2 x 8½in (21.6cm)
M	3	5½in x 45½in (14cm x 115.6cm)	10	2 x 45½in (115.6cm)	2 x 8½in (21.6cm)
Round 4 (clockwise) * see note below			**Completed size: 66½in (168.9cm) square**		
N	4 *	6½in x 45½in (16.5cm x 115.6cm)	6	2 x 45½in (115.6cm)	2 x 9½in (24.1cm)
O	4 *	6½in x 54½in (16.5cm x 138.4cm)	12	2 x 54½in (138.4cm)	2 x 9½in (24.1cm)
P	4 *	6½in x 54½in (16.5cm x 138.4cm)	6	2 x 54½in (138.4cm)	2 x 9½in (24.1cm)
Q	4 *	6½in x 63½in (16.5cm x 161.3cm)	9	2 x 63½in (161.3cm)	2 x 9½in (24.1cm)
Round 5 (clockwise) # see note below			**Completed size 86½in (219.7cm) square**		
R	5 #	7½in x 63½in (19.1cm x 161.3cm)	13	2 x 63½in (161.3cm)	2 x 10½in (26.7cm)
S	5 #	7½in x 73½in (19.1cm x 186.7cm)	8	2 x 73½in (186.7cm)	2 x 10½in (26.7cm)
T	5 #	7½in x 73½in (19.1cm x 186.7cm)	13	2 x 73½in (186.7cm)	2 x 10½in (26.7cm)
U	5 #	7½in x 83½in (19.1cm x 212.1cm)	6	2 x 83½in (212.1cm)	2 x 10½in (26.7cm)

* Note for Round 4: Cut Fabric 4 for the logs down the length of the fabric, parallel with the selvedge. This allows you to select the fullest flower sections for the logs. Extra fabric has been allowed for this.

 # Note for Round 5: Fabric 5 is very large scale. Cut strips selvedge to selvedge and match the pattern as best as possible for the lengths needed for each border. The pattern will not match exactly. The overall pattern is wavy so when cut there will be a bulge that goes in one direction. When sewing strips end to end, make sure the bulge goes in the same direction and seam it at a spot that comes close to matching the pattern. About 6in (15.2cm) at the end of each strip will be wasted. Remove selvedges from the 9 strips; cut and sew end to end as described above. Then cut the lengths as in the Cutting Table.

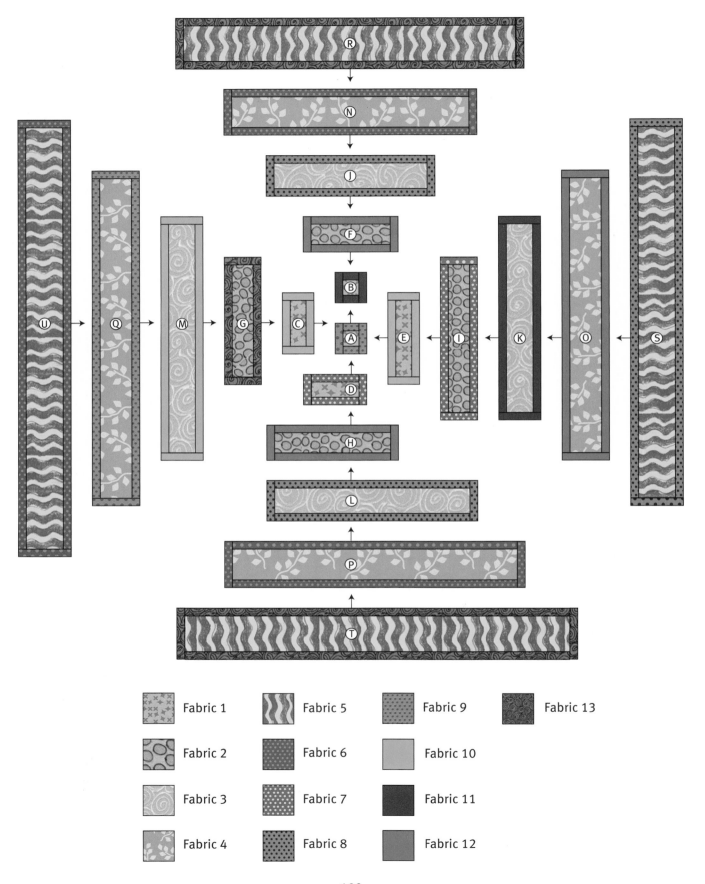

Fabric 1
Fabric 2
Fabric 3
Fabric 4
Fabric 5
Fabric 6
Fabric 7
Fabric 8
Fabric 9
Fabric 10
Fabric 11
Fabric 12
Fabric 13

sun and sea **

Liza Prior Lucy

This quilt of Liza's reminds me of platters of summer fruits beside a rippling sea. The block is a traditional Perkiomen Valley block, also called a split 9-patch. Liza chose the colours of the Adriatic island where this book has been photographed. The quilt is scrappy so there is no need to place each fabric as in the original. Just keep the yellow fabrics in the yellow areas and the blue ones in the blue areas, using red centres as a focal point in each block

SIZE OF FINISHED QUILT
72in x 90in (183cm x 229cm)

FABRICS
Fabrics have been calculated at a maximum width of 40in (102cm), and are cut across the width, unless otherwise stated. Fabrics have been given a number – see Fabric Swatch Diagram for details. As this is a scrappy quilt, we have grouped the fabrics in groups of yellow and blue.

Patchwork Fabrics
GEODES

| Fabric 1 | Red | ⅝yd (60cm) |

Yellow Fabrics Group

| For each fabric: | | ⅜yd (40cm) |

GEODES
| Fabric 2 | Gold |
COLEUS
| Fabric 3 | Yellow |
BRASSICA
| Fabric 4 | Yellow |
ROSE AND HYDRANGEA
| Fabric 5 | Citrus |
PAPER FANS
| Fabric 6 | Yellow |
SPOT
| Fabric 7 | Yellow |
| Fabric 8 | Apple |
ABORIGINAL DOT
| Fabric 9 | Gold |
GUINEA FLOWER
| Fabric 10 | Gold |
BANG
| Fabric 11 | Yellow |

Blue Fabrics Group

| For each fabric: | | ⅜yd (40cm) |

JUMBLE
| Fabric 12 | Duck Egg |
| Fabric 13 | Cobalt |
DIAMOND STRIPE
| Fabric 14 | Blue |
PAPERWEIGHT
| Fabric 15 | Blue |

SPOT
Fabric 16	China Blue
Fabric 17	Turquoise
Fabric 18	Storm
Fabric 19	Duck Egg
ABORIGINAL DOT
Fabric 20	Turquoise
GUINEA FLOWER
Fabric 21	Blue
PAPER FANS
Fabric 22	Cool
Fabric 23	Delft

Border Fabric
PROMENADE STRIPE
| Fabric 24 | Sunny | 2⅛yd (2m) |

Backing and Binding Fabrics
GUINEA FLOWER
| Fabric 25 | Gold | 5½yd (5.1m) |
ABORIGINAL DOT
| Fabric 20 | Turquoise | ¾yd (70cm) |

Batting
80in x 99in (203cm x 249cm)

PATCHES
Each block is made of squares and triangles from strips cut across the width of the fabric. Including the corner blocks, it comprises 52 split 9-patch blocks. Square patches are cut from 3½in (8.9cm) strips. There are 3 yellow squares, 3 blue squares and 1 red square in each block. Triangle patches are cut from 3⅞in (9.8cm) strips, cut diagonally once and paired in yellow and blue combinations to form squares made of 2 half-square triangles (HSTs). There are 2 such squares in each block.

CUTTING OUT
Quilt Centre and Corner Blocks
From Fabric 1 Geodes Red cut 5 strips 3½in (8.9cm) wide and cross cut 52 squares 3½in x 3½in (8.9cm x 8.9cm).

Yellow Fabrics
From each of Fabrics 2–11 cut a strip 3⅞in (9.8cm) wide and cross cut 6 squares 3⅞in x 3⅞in (9.8cm x 9.8cm) from each strip. You need 52 squares in total; 6 from each fabric will give you just more than you need. Cut each square diagonally once to make 2 HSTs. Total of 104 yellow HSTs. Also from each of Fabrics 2–11 cut 2 strips 3½in (8.9cm) wide and cross cut approximately 16 squares 3½in x 3½in (8.9cm x 8.9cm) from each fabric. You can cut 11 squares from a strip. Total of 156 yellow squares.

Blue Fabrics
From each of Fabrics 12–23 cut a strip 3⅞in (9.8cm) wide and cross cut 6 squares 3⅞in x 3⅞in (9.8cm x 9.8cm) from each strip. You need 52 squares in total; 6 from each fabric will give you just more than you need. Cut each square diagonally once to make 2 HSTs from each square. Total of 104 blue HSTs. Also from each of Fabrics 12–23 cut 2 strips 3½in (8.9cm) wide and cross cut approximately 16 squares 3½in x 3½in (8.9cm x 8.9cm) from each fabric. You can cut 11 squares from a strip. Total of 156 blue squares.

Border
From Fabric 24, cutting lengthwise down the fabric, cut 2 lengths 9½in x 72½in (24.1cm x 184cm) and cut 2 lengths 9½in x 54½in (24.1cm x 138.4cm).

Backing
From Fabric 25 cut two lengths approx. 99in (251cm) long, remove selvedges and sew together side to side to make a backing piece approx. 80in x 99in (203cm x 249cm).

Binding
From Fabric 20 cut 9 strips 2½in (6.4cm) wide across the width of fabric. Remove selvedges and sew together end to end.

FABRIC SWATCH DIAGRAM

Patchwork Fabrics

Fabric 1
GEODES
Red
PJ99RD

Fabric 2
GEODES
Gold
PJ99GD

Fabric 3
COLEUS
Yellow
PJ30YE

Fabric 4
BRASSICA
Yellow
PJ51YE

Fabric 5
ROSE AND HYDRANGEA
Citrus
PJ97CT

Fabric 6
PAPER FANS
Yellow
GP143YE

Fabric 7
SPOT
Yellow
GP70YE

Fabric 8
SPOT
Apple
GP70AL

Fabric 9
ABORIGINAL DOT
Gold
GP71GD

Fabric 10
GUINEA FLOWER
Gold
GP59GD

Fabric 11
BANG
Yellow
BM72YE

Fabric 12
JUMBLE
Duck Egg
BM53DE

Fabric 13
JUMBLE
Cobalt
BM53CB

Fabric 14
DIAMOND STRIPE
Blue
GP170BL

Fabric 15
PAPERWEIGHT
Blue
GP20BL

Fabric 16
SPOT
China Blue
GP70CI

Fabric 17
SPOT
Turquoise
GP70TQ

Fabric 18
SPOT
Storm
GP70SR

Fabric 19
SPOT
Duck Egg
GP70DE

Fabric 20
ABORIGINAL DOT
Turquoise
GP71TQ

Fabric 21
GUINEA FLOWER
Blue
GP59BL

Fabric 22
PAPER FANS
Cool
GP143CL

Fabric 23
PAPER FANS
Delft
GP143DF

Border Fabric

Fabric 24
PROMENADE STRIPE
Sunny
GP178SY

Backing and Binding Fabrics

Fabric 25
GUINEA FLOWER
Gold
GP59GD

Fabric 20
ABORIGINAL DOT
Turquoise
GP71TQ

BLOCK ASSEMBLY DIAGRAM

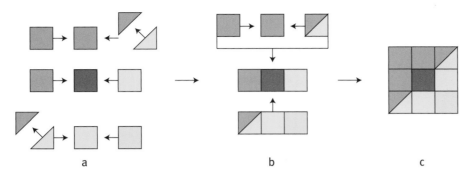

a   b   c

MAKING THE BLOCKS

Using the Block Assembly Diagram as a guide, choose 3 yellow squares, 3 blue squares, a Fabric 1 Red square, 2 yellow triangles and 2 blue triangles. Using a ¼in (6mm) seam allowance throughout, sew the yellow and blue triangles together along their long edge to make 2 HST patches (a). Arrange them with the other squares to form the 9-split patch block (b) and sew together, matching seam joins, to create the finished block (c). Make 52 blocks.

MAKING THE QUILT

Centre Blocks

Using the Quilt Assembly Diagram and the photograph as a guide, arrange the blocks on a design wall with the blue halves facing the correct direction to form the radiating blue and yellow squares. Re-arrange if neccessary to avoid the same fabrics meeting in neighbouring blocks. Sew the centre blocks together in rows of 6. Press and sew the 8 rows together.

Border

Position the corner blocks and border pieces around the quilt centre and check your layout. Pin and sew the long side borders to the quilt centre. Sew the corner blocks to each end of the shorter top and bottom borders, taking care to check the blocks are positioned with the yellow halves towards the quilt centre as shown in the Quilt Assembly Diagram. Pin and sew the top and bottom borders to the quilt.

FINISHING THE QUILT

Press the quilt top. Layer the quilt top, batting and backing, and baste together (see page 140).
Quilt as desired.
Trim the quilt edges and attach the binding (see page 141).

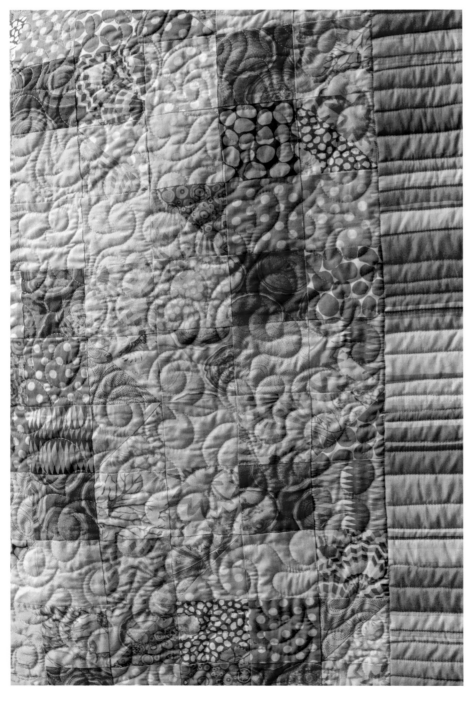

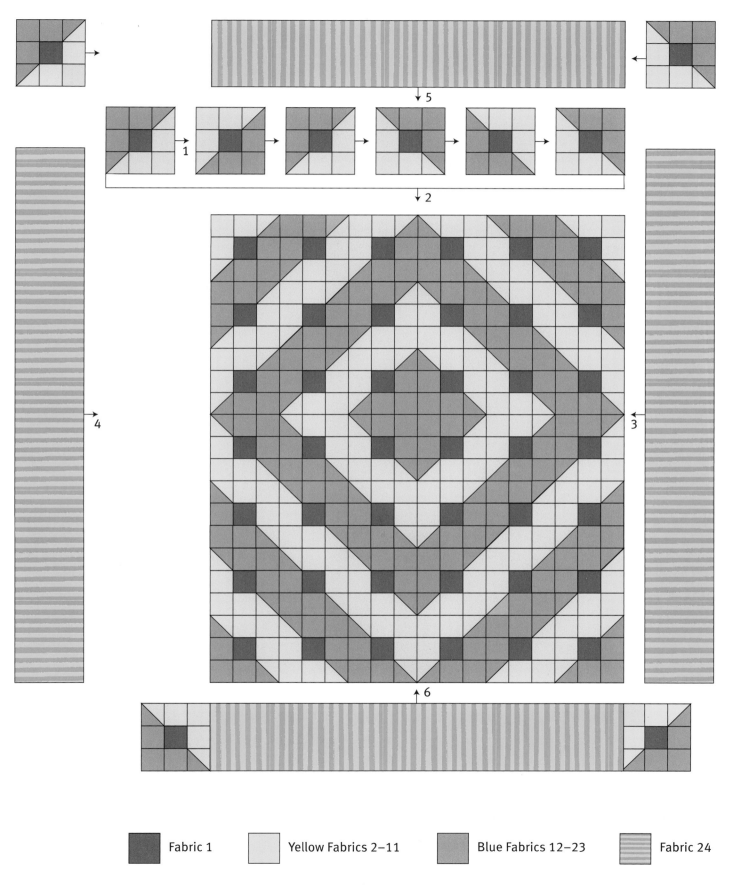

Fabric 1   Yellow Fabrics 2–11   Blue Fabrics 12–23   Fabric 24

turkish coffee **

Liza Prior Lucy

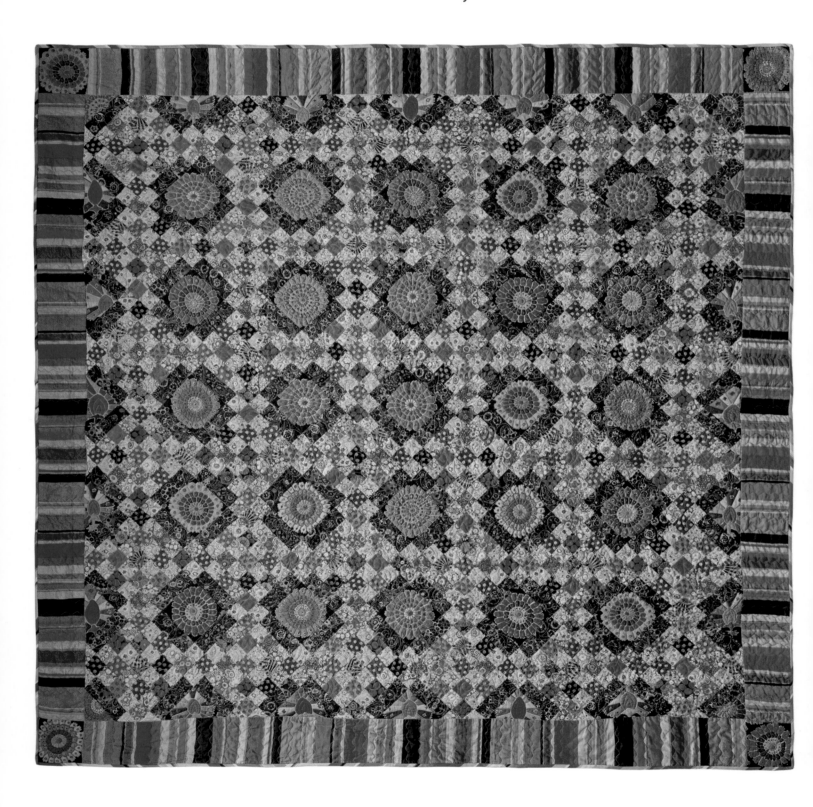

Bravo, Liza! The dramatic, dark, Turkish Delight print, fussy cut, makes this simple-to-construct quilt a wonder to study. The dark stripe border works a treat as well. As this is a scrappy quilt, it is not necessary to place each of the fabrics, or the Turkish Delight motifs, exactly as in the original. The smaller-scale mid-toned prints against the dark Millefiore fabric make striking shadows.

SIZE OF FINISHED QUILT
85½in x 85½in (217cm x 217cm)

FABRICS
Fabrics have been calculated at a maximum width of 40in (102cm), and are cut across the width, unless otherwise stated. Fabrics have been given a number – see Fabric Swatch Diagram for details.

Patchwork Fabrics
TURKISH DELIGHT
Fabric 1	Black	3yd (2.8m)
MILLEFIORE
Fabric 2	Dark	1½yd (1.4m)
Fabric 3	Antique	2½yd (2.3m)
PAPER FANS
Fabric 4	Black	¼yd (25cm)
PAPERWEIGHT
Fabric 5	Purple	¼yd (25cm)
ROMAN GLASS
Fabric 6	Purple	¼yd (25cm)
ROW FLOWERS
Fabric 7	Dark	¼yd (25cm)
ABORIGINAL DOT
Fabric 8	Periwinkle	¼yd (25cm)
SPOT
Fabric 9	Black	¼yd (25cm)
Fabric 10	Bottle	¼yd (25cm)
Fabric 11	Burgundy	¼yd (25cm)
Fabric 12	Peacock	¼yd (25cm)
Fabric 13	Violet	¼yd (25cm)
JUMBLE
Fabric 14	Blue	¼yd (25cm)
PROMENADE STRIPE
Fabric 15	Dark	2½yd (2.3m)

Backing and Binding Fabrics
JAPANESE CHRYSANTHEMUM
Fabric 16	Antique	7yd (6.5m)
PROMENADE STRIPE
Fabric 17	Cold	¾yd (70cm)

Batting
94in x 94in (239cm x 239cm)

FABRIC SWATCH DIAGRAM

Patchwork Fabrics

Fabric 1
TURKISH DELIGHT
Black
GP81BK

Fabric 2
MILLEFIORE
Dark
GP92DK

Fabric 3
MILLEFIORE
Antique
GP92AN

Fabrics 4
PAPER FANS
Black
GP143BK

Fabric 5
PAPERWEIGHT
Purple
GP20PU

Fabric 6
ROMAN GLASS
Purple
GP01PU

Fabric 7
ROW FLOWERS
Dark
GP169DK

Fabric 8
ABORIGINAL DOT
Periwinkle
GP71PE

Fabric 9
SPOT
Black
GP70BK

Fabric 10
SPOT
Bottle
GP70BT

Fabric 11
SPOT
Burgundy
GP70BG

Fabric 12
SPOT
Peacock
GP70PC

Fabric 13
SPOT
Violet
GP70VI

Fabric 14
JUMBLE
Blue
BM53BL

Fabric 15
PROMENADE STRIPE
Dark
GP178DK

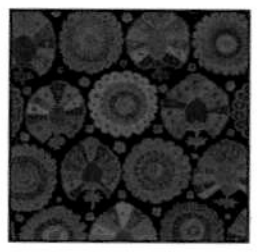

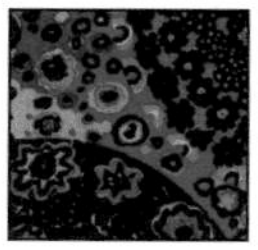

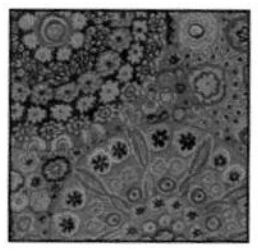

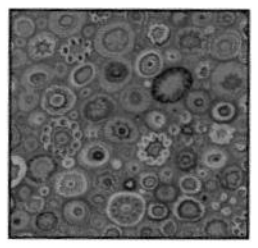

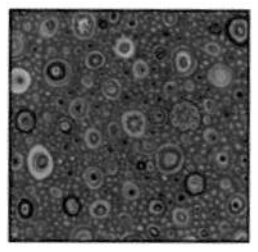

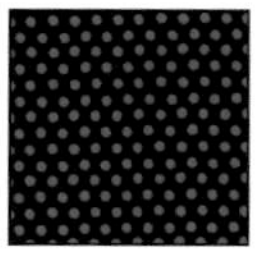

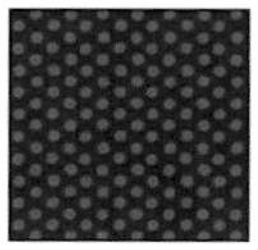

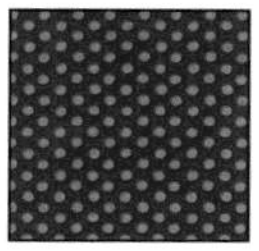

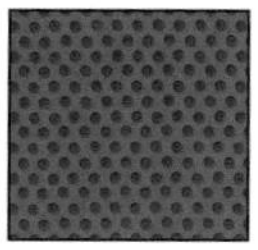

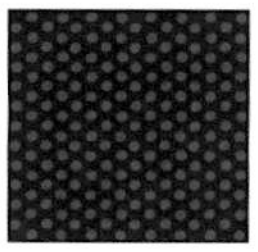

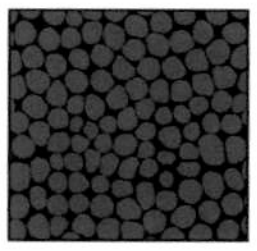

Backing and Binding Fabrics

Fabric 16
JAPANESE CHRYSANTHEMUM
Antique
PJ41AN

Fabric 17
PROMENADE STRIPE
Cold
GP178CD

TEMPLATES

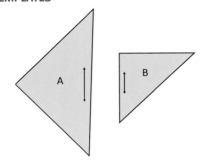

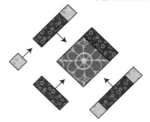

Feature Motif Block

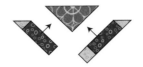

Side Triangle

Corner Triangle

PATCHES

Feature patches are fussy-cut squares and triangles cut from Fabric 1. Triangles are fussy cut using Templates A and B. Remaining patches are squares and rectangles cut from strips cut across the width of the fabric.

CUTTING OUT

From Fabric 1 fussy cut the following patches:

Border corner squares 4 squares 6in x 6in (15.2cm x 15.2cm) with a round motif centred in each square.

Feature squares 25 squares 5¾in x 5¾in (14.6cm x 14.6cm) with a round motif centred in each square.

Side triangles Use Template A to fussy cut 20 side triangles, positioning an arched motif in each triangle. Use the photograph to see how best to cut them for each of the 4 sides.

Corner triangles Use Template B to fussy cut 4 partial-round motifs for the corners.

From Fabric 2 cut 9 strips 5¾in (14.6cm) wide across the width of the fabric. Cross cut 17 rectangles 2¼in (5.7cm) wide from each strip. Cut a total of 144 rectangles 2¼in x 5¾in (5.7cm x 14.6cm).

From Fabric 3 cut 2 strips 3¾in (9.5cm) wide and cross cut 12 squares 3¾in (9.5cm) square. Cut each square diagonally twice to make 48 quarter-square triangles. Cut 33 strips 2¼in (5.7cm) wide and cross cut 552 squares 2¼in (5.7cm) square. (You can cut 17 squares from each strip.)

From each of Fabrics 4, 5, 6, 7, 8, 9, 10, 11, 12, 13 and 14 cut 3 strips 2¼in (5.7cm) wide. Cross cut 43 squares 2¼in (5.7cm) square from each fabric. Total of 468 squares 2¼in (5.7cm) square. (You can cut 17 squares from each strip.)

From Fabric 15 cut 4 lengths down the length of the fabric (parallel with the selvedge) 6in x 74¾in (15.2cm x 189.9cm).

Backing

From Fabric 16 cut two 94in (239cm) lengths. From the remaining yardage, cut 2 panels 17in x 48in (43cm x 122cm). Remove the selvedges. Sew the two smaller panels end to end and trim to 94in (239cm). Place that panel between the larger panels and sew together to make a backing approximately 94in x 94in (239cm x 239cm).

Binding

From Fabric 17 cut 9 strips 2½in (6.4cm) wide. Sew end to end (see page 141).

MAKING THE BLOCKS

Use a ¼in (6mm) seam allowance throughout.

There are two blocks: feature motif blocks and checkerboard blocks.

Feature Motif Blocks

Referring to the Feature Motif Block Assembly Diagram, sew a Fabric 2 rectangle to opposite sides of a Fabric 1 square. Sew Fabric 3 squares to each end of 2 more Fabric 2 rectangles, then sew those to the other two sides of the Fabric 1 square. For the side triangles, keeping in mind the direction of the Fabric 1 motif for each of the 4 sides, sew a Fabric 3 quarter-square triangle to a Fabric 2 rectangle and sew onto a short edge of a side triangle. Sew a Fabric 3 square to one end and a quarter-square triangle to the other end of a Fabric 2 rectangle and sew to the other short edge of the side triangle.

For the corner triangles, sew a quarter-square triangle to each end of a Fabric 2 rectangle, then sew to the long edge of a Fabric 1 corner triangle.

CHECKERBOARD BLOCK ASSEMBLY DIAGRAM

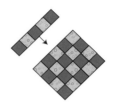

Checkerboard Blocks

Make sure each block has a good selection of different dark squares from Fabrics 4–14 and that a dark square is positioned at each corner.

Referring to the Checkerboard Block Assembly Diagram, make up 36 checkerboard 5-square blocks with 5 rows of 5 squares using 12 light squares from Fabric 3 and 13 dark squares randomly chosen from Fabrics 4–14. Sew the blocks into 5 rows then sew the rows together.

MAKING THE QUILT

Lay out the blocks on point in rows using the photograph and Quilt Assembly Diagram as guides, taking care to orientate the blocks on each side correctly. Use a ¼in (6mm) seam allowance throughout. Sew the blocks into diagonal rows. Sew borders to both sides. Sew the 4 larger Fabric 1 feature motif squares to each end of the remaining two borders, then pin and sew to the top and bottom.

FINISHING THE QUILT

Layer the quilt top, batting and backing, and baste together (see page 140). Quilt as desired. Trim the quilt edges and attach the binding (see page 141).

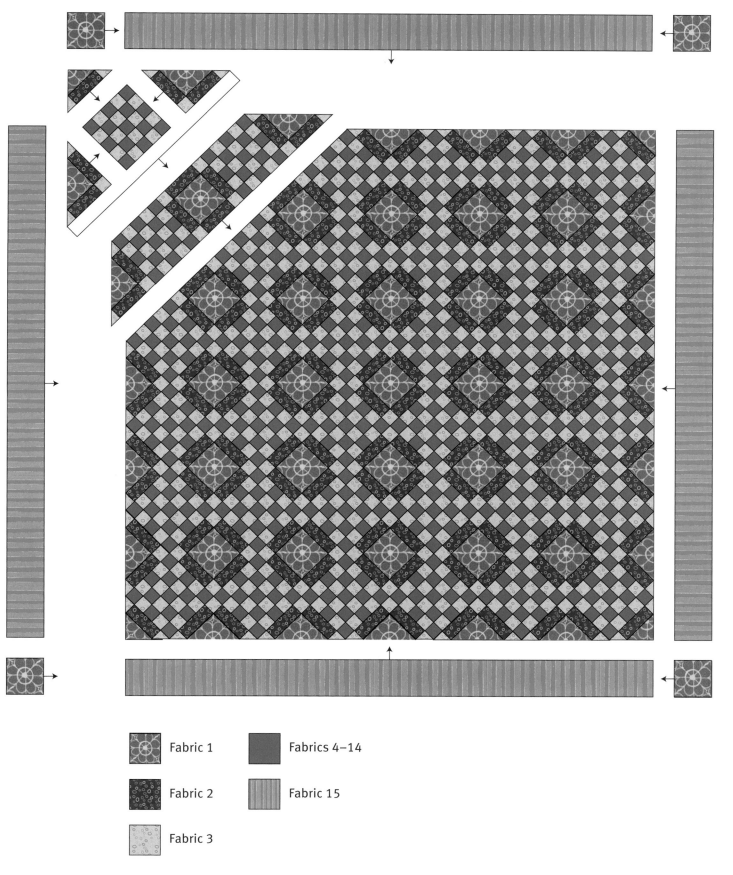

Fabric 1

Fabrics 4–14

Fabric 2

Fabric 15

Fabric 3

templates

Refer to the individual quilt instructions for the templates needed. Look for the quilt name on the templates to make sure you are using the correct shapes for the project. Arrows on templates should be lined up with the straight grain of the fabric, which runs either along the selvedge or at 90 degrees to the selvedge. Following marked grain lines is important to avoid bias edges, which can cause distortion.

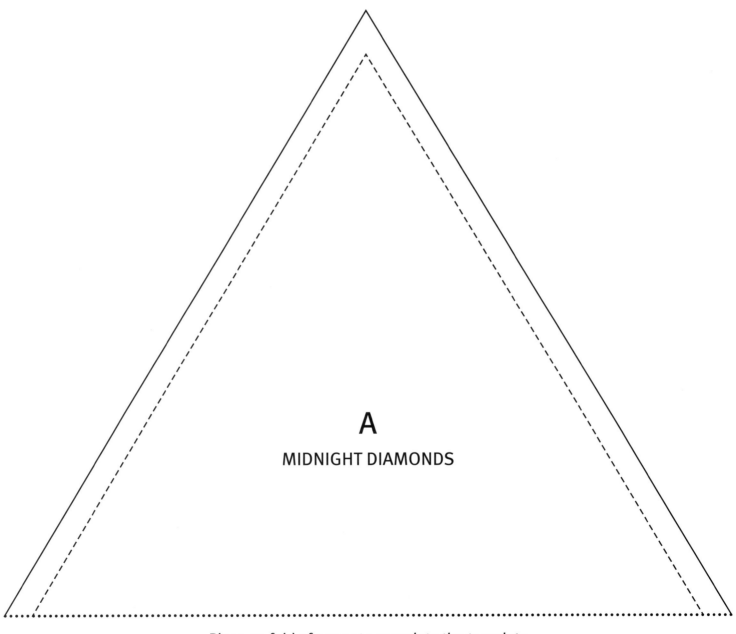

A
MIDNIGHT DIAMONDS

Place on fold of paper to complete the template

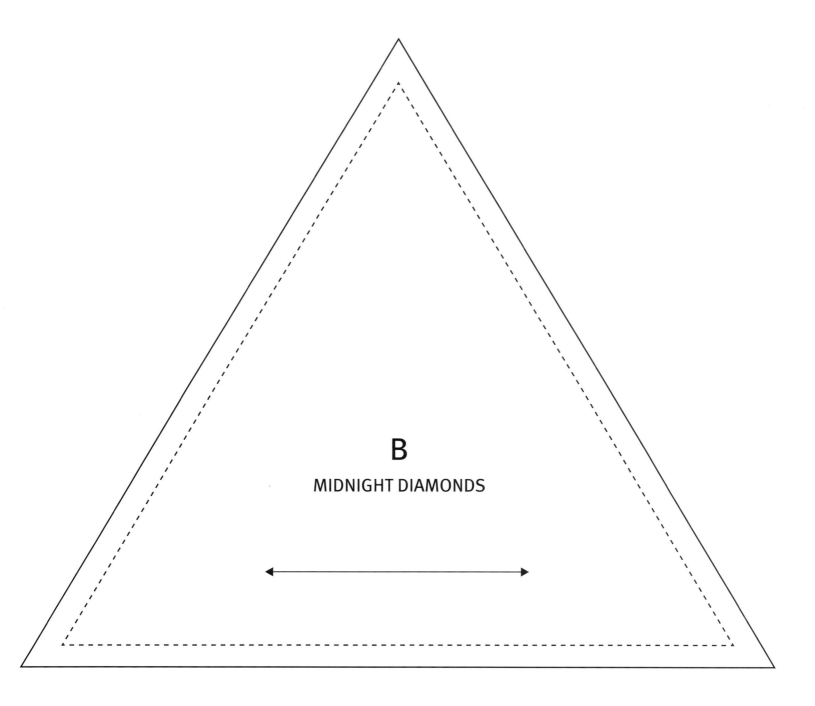

B

MIDNIGHT DIAMONDS

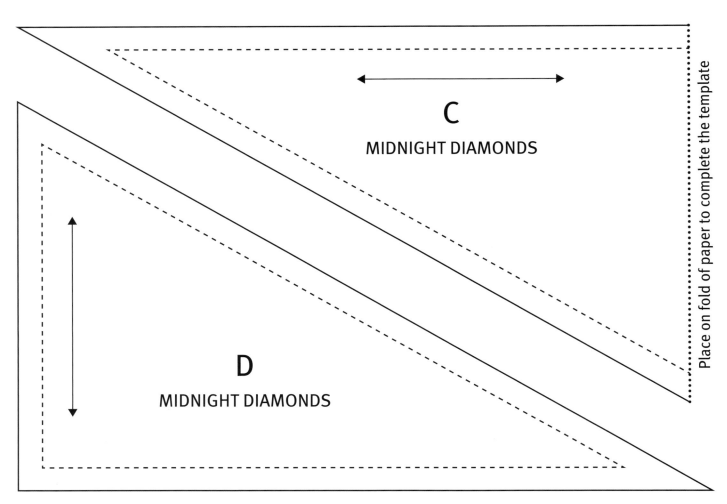

C

MIDNIGHT DIAMONDS

Place on fold of paper to complete the template

D

MIDNIGHT DIAMONDS

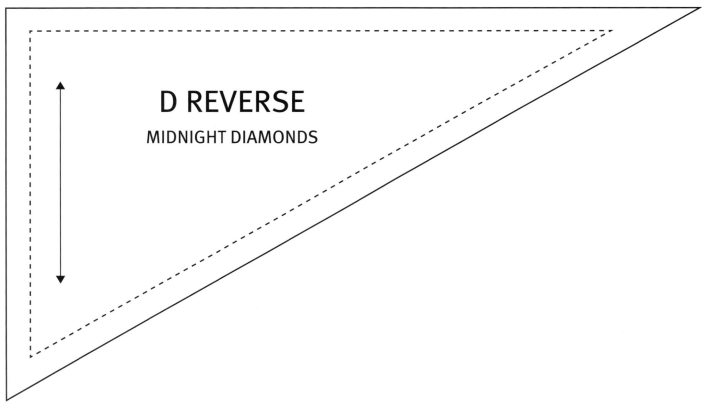

D REVERSE

MIDNIGHT DIAMONDS

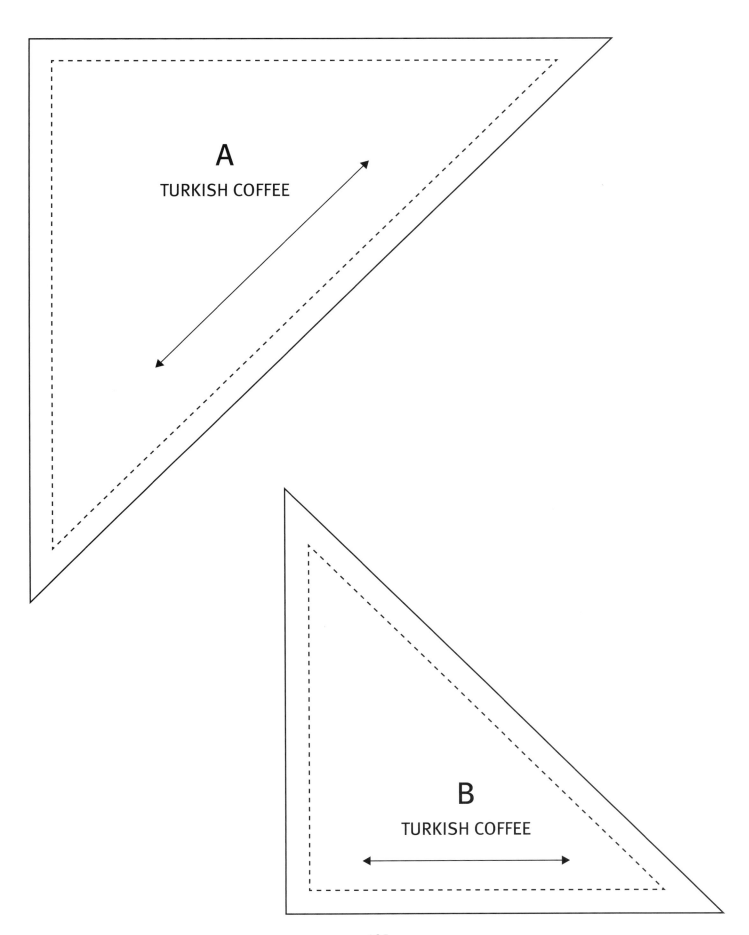

A

TURKISH COFFEE

B

TURKISH COFFEE

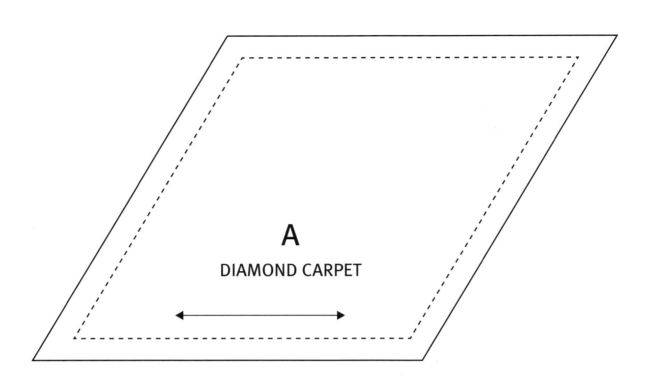

A

DIAMOND CARPET

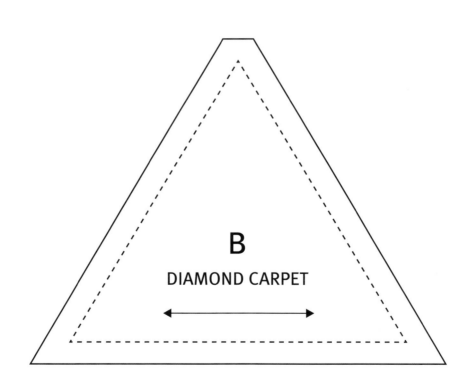

B

DIAMOND CARPET

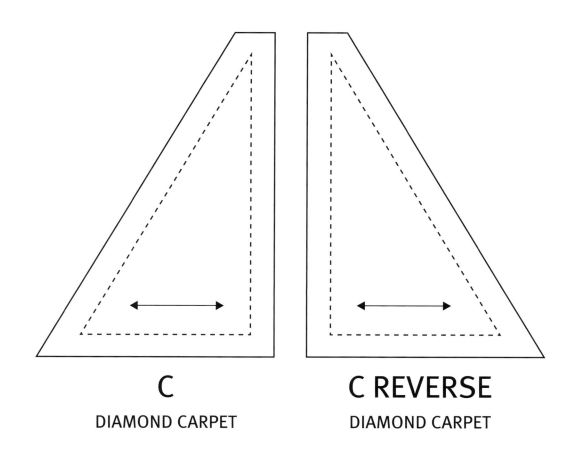

C
DIAMOND CARPET

C REVERSE
DIAMOND CARPET

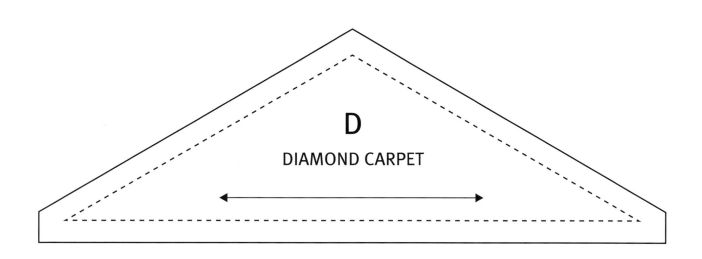

D
DIAMOND CARPET

patchwork and quilting know-how

These instructions are intended for the novice quilt maker, providing the basic information needed to make the projects in this book, along with some useful tips.

EXPERIENCE RATINGS
* Easy, straightforward, suitable for a beginner.
** Suitable for the average patchworker and quilter.
*** For the more experienced patchworker and quilter.

ABOUT THE FABRICS
The fabrics used for the quilts in this book are mainly from Kaffe Fassett Collective:
GP is the code for Kaffe Fassett's designs, PJ for Philip Jacobs' and BM for Brandon Mably's. The other fabrics used are Kaffe Fassett's Sew Artisan. The prefix PWKF is for the prints and the prefix PWBK is for the batiks.

PREPARING THE FABRIC
Prewash all new fabrics before you begin, to ensure that there will be no uneven shrinkage and no bleeding of colours when the finished quilt is laundered. Press the fabric whilst it is still damp to return crispness to it. All fabric requirements in this book are calculated on a 40in (102cm) usable fabric width, to allow for shrinkage and selvedge removal.

MAKING TEMPLATES
Transparent template plastic is the best material to use: it is durable and allows you to see the fabric and select certain motifs. You can also use tracing paper and thin stiff cardboard.

Templates for machine piecing
1 Trace off the actual-sized template provided either directly on to template plastic, or on to tracing paper and then on to thin cardboard. Use a ruler to help you trace off the straight cutting line, dotted seam line and grain lines.
   Sometimes templates are too large to print complete. Transfer the template on to the fold of a large sheet of paper, cut out and open out for the full template.
2 Cut out the traced off template using a craft knife, a ruler and a self-healing cutting mat.
3 Punch holes in the corners of the template, at each point on the seam line, using a hole punch.

Templates for hand piecing
• Make a template as for machine piecing, but do not trace off the cutting line. Use the dotted seam line as the outer edge of the template.

• This template allows you to draw the seam lines directly on to the fabric. The seam allowances can then be cut by eye around the patch.

CUTTING THE FABRIC
On the individual instructions for each project, you will find a summary of all the patch shapes used.
   Always mark and cut out any border and binding strips first, followed by the largest patch shapes and finally the smallest ones, to make the most efficient use of your fabric. The border and binding strips are best cut using a rotary cutter.

Rotary cutting
Rotary cut strips are usually cut across the fabric from selvedge to selvedge, but some projects may vary, so please read through all the instructions before you start cutting the fabrics.

1 Before beginning to cut, press out any folds or creases in the fabric. If you are cutting a large piece of fabric, you will need to fold it several times to fit the cutting mat. When there is only a single fold, place the fold facing you. If the fabric is too wide to be folded only once, fold it concertina-style until it fits your mat. A small rotary cutter with a sharp blade will cut up to six layers of fabric; a large cutter up to eight layers.

2 To ensure that your cut strips are straight and even, the folds must be placed exactly parallel to the straight edges of the fabric and along a line on the cutting mat.

3 Place a plastic ruler over the raw edge of the fabric, overlapping it about ½in (1.25cm). Make sure that the ruler is at right angles to both the straight edges and the fold to ensure that you cut along the straight grain. Press down on the ruler and wheel the cutter away from you along the edge of the ruler.

4 Open out the fabric to check the edge. Don't worry if it's not perfectly straight – a little wiggle will not show when the quilt is stitched together. Re-fold the fabric, then place the ruler over the trimmed edge, aligning the edge with the markings on the ruler that match the correct strip width. Cut strip along the edge of the ruler.

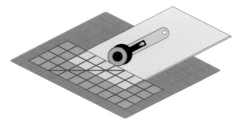

USING TEMPLATES
The most efficient way to cut out templates is by first rotary cutting a strip of fabric to the width stated for your template, and then marking off your templates along the strip, edge to edge at the required angle. This method leaves hardly any waste and gives a random effect to your patches.
   A less efficient method is to fussy cut them, where the templates are cut individually by placing them on particular motifs or stripes, to create special effects. Although this method is more wasteful, it yields very interesting results.

1 Place the template face down, on the wrong side of the fabric, with the grain-line arrow following the straight grain of the fabric, if indicated. Be careful though – check with your individual instructions, as some instructions may ask you to cut patches on varying grains.

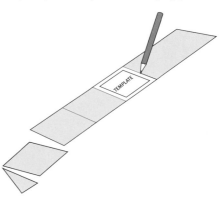

2 Hold the template firmly in place and draw around it with a sharp pencil or crayon, marking in the corner dots or seam lines. To save fabric, position patches close together or even touching. Don't worry if outlines positioned on the straight grain when drawn on striped fabrics do not always match the stripes when cut – this will add a degree of visual excitement to the patchwork!

3 Once you've drawn all the pieces needed, you are ready to cut the fabric, with either a rotary cutter and ruler or a pair of sharp sewing scissors.

BASIC HAND AND MACHINE PIECING
Patches can be stitched together by hand or machine. Machine stitching is quicker, but hand assembly allows you to carry your patches around with you and work on them in every spare moment. The choice is yours. For techniques that are new to you, practise on scrap pieces of fabric until you feel confident.

Machine piecing

Follow the quilt instructions for the order in which to piece the individual patchwork blocks and then assemble the blocks together in rows.

1 Seam lines are not marked on the fabric for simple shapes, so stitch ¼in (6mm) seams using the machine needle plate, a ¼in (6mm) wide machine foot, or tape stuck to the machine as a guide. Pin two patches with right sides together, matching edges.

For some shapes, particularly diamonds, you need to match the sewing lines, not the fabric edges. Place 2 diamonds right sides together but offset so that the sewing lines intersect at the correct position. Use pins to secure for sewing.

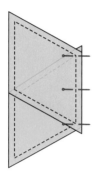

Set your machine at 10–12 stitches per inch (2.5cm) and stitch seams from edge to edge, removing pins as you feed the fabric through the machine.

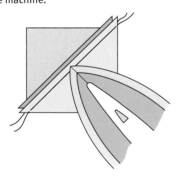

2 Press the seams of each patchwork block to one side before attempting to join it to another block. When joining diamond shaped blocks you will need to offset the blocks in the same way as diamond shaped patches, matching the sewing lines, not the fabric edges.

3 When joining rows of blocks, make sure that adjacent seam allowances are pressed in opposite directions to reduce bulk and make matching easier. Pin pieces together directly through the stitch line and to the right and left of the seam. Remove pins as you sew. Continue pressing seams to one side as you work.

Hand piecing

1 Pin two patches with right sides together, so that the marked seam lines are facing outwards.

2 Using a single strand of strong thread, secure the corner of a seam line with a couple of back stitches.

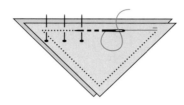

3 Sew running stitches along the marked line, working 8–10 stitches per inch (2.5cm) and ending at the opposite seam line corner with a few back stitches. When hand piecing never stitch over the seam allowances.

4 Press the seams to one side, as shown in machine piecing (Step 2).

MACHINE APPLIQUÉ WITH ADHESIVE WEB

To make appliqué very easy you can use adhesive web (which comes attached to a paper backing sheet) to bond the motifs to the background fabric. There are two types of web available: the first keeps the pieces in place while they are stitched, the second permanently attaches the pieces so that no sewing is required. Follow steps 1 and 2 for the non-sew type and steps 1–3 for the type that requires sewing.

1 Trace the reversed appliqué design onto the paper side of the adhesive web, leaving a ¼in (6mm) gap between all the shapes. Roughly cut out the motifs ⅛in (3mm) outside your drawn line.

2 Bond the motifs to the reverse of your chosen fabrics. Cut out on the drawn line with very sharp scissors. Remove the backing paper by scoring the centre of the motif carefully with a scissor point and peeling the paper away from the centre out (to prevent damage to the edges). Place the motifs onto the background, noting any which may be layered. Cover with a clean cloth and bond with a hot iron (check instructions for temperature setting as adhesive web can vary depending on the manufacturer).

3 Using a contrasting or toning coloured thread in your machine, work small close zig zag stitches (or a blanket stitch if your machine has one) around the edge of the

motifs; the majority of the stitching should sit on the appliqué shape. When stitching up to points, stop with the machine needle in the down position, lift the foot of your machine, pivot the work, lower the foot and continue to stitch. Make sure all the raw edges are stitched.

HAND APPLIQUÉ

Good preparation is essential for speedy and accurate hand appliqué. The finger-pressing method is suitable for needle-turning application, used for simple shapes like leaves and flowers. Using a card template is the best method for bold simple motifs such as circles.

Finger–pressing method

1 To make your template, transfer the appliqué design using carbon paper on to stiff card, and cut out the template. Trace around the outline of your appliquéd shape on to the right side of your fabric using a well sharpened pencil. Cut out shapes, adding by eye a ¼in (6mm) seam allowance all around.

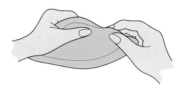

2 Hold the shape right side up and fold under the seam, turning along your drawn line, pinch to form a crease. Dampening the fabric makes this very easy. When using shapes with points such as leaves, turn in the seam allowance at the point first, as shown in the diagram. Then continue all round the shape. If your shapes have sharp curves, you can snip the seam allowance to ease the curve. Take care not to stretch the appliqué shapes as you work.

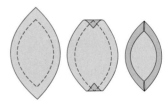

Straight stems

Place fabric face down and simply press over the ¼in (6mm) seam allowance along each edge. You don't need to finish the ends of stems that are layered under other appliqué shapes. Where the end of the stem is visible, simply tuck under the end and finish neatly.

Needle-turning application

Take the appliqué shape and pin in position. Stroke the seam allowance under with the tip of the needle as far as the creased pencil line, and hold securely in place with your thumb. Using a matching thread, bring the needle up from the back of the block into the edge of the shape and proceed to blind-hem in place. (This stitch allows the motifs to appear to be held on invisibly.) To do this, bring the thread out from below through the folded edge of the motif, never on the top. The stitches must be small, even and close together to prevent the seam allowance from unfolding and from frayed edges appearing. Try to avoid pulling the stitches too tight, as this will cause the motifs to pucker up. Work around the whole shape, stroking under each small section before sewing.

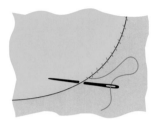

QUILTING
When you have finished piecing your patchwork and added any borders, press it carefully. It is now ready for quilting.

Marking quilting designs and motifs
Many tools are available for marking quilting patterns, check the manufacturer's instructions for use and test on scraps of fabric from your project. Use an acrylic ruler for marking straight lines.

Stencils
Some designs require stencils, these can be made at home, by transferring the designs on to template plastic, or stiff cardboard. The design is then cut away in the form of long dashes, to act as guides for both internal and external lines. These stencils are a quick method for producing an identical set of repeated designs.

BACKING FABRIC
The quilts in this book use two different widths of backing fabric – the standard width of 44in (112cm) and a wider one of 108in (274cm). If you can't find (or don't want to use) the wider fabric then select a standard-width fabric instead and adjust the amount accordingly. For most of the quilts in the book, using a standard-width fabric will probably mean joins in the fabric. The material list for each quilt assumes that an extra 4in of backing fabric is needed all round (8in in total) when making up the quilt sandwich, to allow for long-arm quilting if needed. We have assumed a usable width of 40in (102cm), to allow for selvedge removal and possible shrinkage after washing.

Preparing the backing and batting
• Remove the selvedges and piece together the backing fabric to form a backing at least 4in (10cm) larger all around than the patchwork top.

• Choose a fairly thin batting, preferably pure cotton, to give your quilt a flat appearance. If your batting has been rolled up, unroll it and let it rest before cutting it to the same size as the backing.

• For a large quilt it may be necessary to join two pieces of batting to fit. Lay the pieces of batting on a flat surface so that they overlap by around 8in (20cm). Cut a curved line through both layers.

overlap wadding

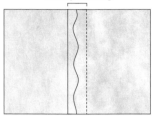

• Carefully peel away the two narrow pieces and discard. Butt the curved cut edges back together. Stitch the two pieces together using a large herringbone stitch.

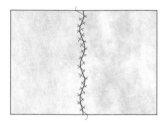

BASTING THE LAYERS TOGETHER
1 On the floor or on a large work surface, lay out the backing with wrong side uppermost. Use weights along the edges to keep it taut.

2 Lay the batting on the backing and smooth it out gently. Next lay the patchwork top, right side up, on top of the batting and smooth gently until there are no wrinkles. Pin at the corners and at the midpoints of each side, close to the edges.

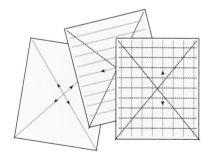

3 Beginning at the centre, baste diagonal lines outwards to the corners, making your stitches about 3in (7.5cm) long. Then, again starting at the centre, baste horizontal and vertical lines out to the edges. Continue basting until you have basted a grid of lines about 4in (10cm) apart over the entire quilt.

4 For speed, when machine quilting, some quilters prefer to baste their quilt sandwich layers together using rust-proof safety pins, spaced at 4in (10cm) intervals over the entire quilt.

HAND QUILTING
This is best done with the quilt mounted on a quilting frame or hoop, but as long as you have basted the quilt well, a frame is not essential. With the quilt top facing upwards, begin at the centre of the quilt and make even running stitches following the design. It is more important to make even stitches on both sides of the quilt than to make small ones. Start and finish your stitching with back stitches and bury the ends of your threads in the batting.

TIED QUILTING
If you prefer you could use tied quilting rather than machine quilting. For tied quilting, use a strong thread that will withstand being pulled through the quilt layers and tied in a knot. You can tie with the knot on the front of the quilt or the back, as preferred. Leaving tufts of thread gives an attractive, rustic look.

Thread a needle with a suitable thread, using the number of strands noted in the project. Put the needle and thread through from the front of the work, leaving a long tail. Go through to the back of the quilt, make a small stitch and then come back through to the front. Tie the threads together using a reef knot and trim the thread ends to the desired length. For extra security, you could tie a double knot or add a spot of fabric glue on the knot.

MACHINE QUILTING

• For a flat looking quilt, always use a walking foot on your machine for stitching straight lines, and a darning foot for free-motion quilting.

• It is best to start your quilting at the centre of the quilt and work out towards the borders, doing the straight quilting lines first (stitch-in-the-ditch) followed by the free-motion quilting.

• When free-motion quilting, stitch in a loose meandering style as shown in the diagrams. Do not stitch too closely as this will make the quilt feel stiff when finished. If you wish you can include floral themes or follow shapes on the printed fabrics for added interest.

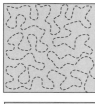

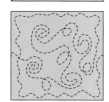

• Make it easier for yourself by handling the quilt properly. Roll up the excess quilt neatly to fit under your sewing machine arm, and use a table or chair to help support the weight of the quilt that hangs down the other side.

FINISHING

Preparing to bind the edges

Once you have quilted or tied your quilt sandwich together, remove all the basting stitches. Then, baste around the outer edge of the quilt ¼in (6mm) from the edge of the top patchwork layer. Trim the back and batting to the edge of the patchwork and straighten the edge of the patchwork if necessary.

Making the binding

1 Cut bias or straight grain strips the width required for your binding, making sure the grain-line is running the correct way on your straight grain strips. Cut enough strips until you have the required length to go around the edge of your quilt.

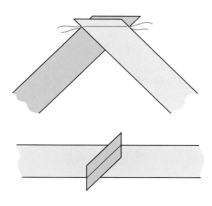

2 To join strips together, the two ends that are to be joined must be cut at a 45 degree angle, as above. Stitch right sides together, trim turnings and press seam open.

Binding the edges

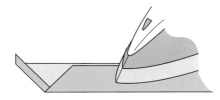

1 Cut the starting end of binding strip at a 45 degree angle, fold a ¼in (6mm) turning to wrong side along cut edge and press in place. With wrong sides together, fold strip in half lengthways, keeping raw edges level, and press.

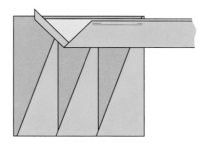

2 Starting at the centre of one of the long edges, place the doubled binding on to the right side of the quilt keeping raw edges level. Stitch the binding in place. starting ¼in (6mm) in from the diagonal folded edge. Reverse stitch to secure, and work ¼in (6mm) in from edge of the quilt towards first corner of quilt. Stop ¼in (6mm) in from corner and work a few reverse stitches.

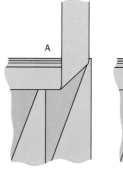

3 Fold the loose end of the binding up, making a 45 degree angle (see A). Keeping the diagonal fold in place, fold the binding back down, aligning the raw edges with the next side of the quilt. Starting at the point where the last stitch ended, stitch down the next side (see B).

4 Continue to stitch the binding in place around all the quilt edges in this way, tucking the finishing end of the binding inside the diagonal starting section.

5 Turn the folded edge of the binding on to the back of the quilt. Hand stitch the folded edge in place just covering binding machine stitches, and folding a mitre at each corner.

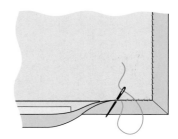

glossary of terms

Adhesive or fusible web This comes attached to a paper-backed sheet and is used to bond appliqué motifs to a background fabric. There are 2 types of web available, the first keeps the pieces in place whilst they are stitched, the second permanently attaches the pieces so that no sewing is required.

Appliqué The technique of stitching fabric shapes on to a background to create a design. It can be applied either by hand or machine with a decorative embroidery stitch, such as buttonhole, or satin stitch.

Backing The bottom layer of a quilt sandwich. It is made of fabric pieced to the size of the quilt top with the addition of about 4in (10cm) all around to allow for quilting take-up.

Basting or tacking This is a means of holding two fabric layers or the layers of a quilt sandwich together temporarily with large hand stitches or pins.

Batting or wadding This is the middle layer, or padding in a quilt. It can be made of cotton, wool, silk or synthetic fibres.

Bias The diagonal grain of a fabric. This is the direction which has the most give or stretch, making it ideal for bindings, especially on curved edges.

Binding A narrow strip of fabric used to finish off the edges of quilts or projects; it can be cut on the straight grain of a fabric or on the bias.

Block A single design unit that when stitched together with other blocks create the quilt top. It is most often a square, hexagon, or rectangle, but it can be any shape. It can be pieced or plain.

Border A frame of fabric stitched to the outer edges of the quilt top. Borders can be narrow or wide, pieced or plain. As well as making the quilt larger, they unify the overall design and draw attention to the central area.

Chalk pencils Available in various colours, they are used for marking lines or spots on fabric.

Cutting mat Designed for use with a rotary cutter, it is made from a special self-healing material that keeps your cutting blade sharp. Cutting mats come in various sizes and are usually marked with a grid to help you line up the edges of fabric and cut out larger pieces.

Design wall Used for laying out fabric patches before sewing. A large wall or folding board covered with flannel fabric or cotton batting in a neutral shade (dull beige or grey work well) will hold fabric in place so that an overall view can be taken of the placement.

Free-motion quilting Curved wavy quilting lines stitched in a random manner. Stitching diagrams are often given for you to follow as a loose guide.

Fussy cutting This is when a template is placed on a particular motif, or stripe, to obtain interesting effects. This method is not as efficient as strip cutting, but yields very interesting results.

Grain The direction in which the threads run in a woven fabric. In a vertical direction it is called the lengthwise grain, which has very little stretch. The horizontal direction, or crosswise grain is slightly stretchy, but diagonally the fabric has a lot of stretch. This grain is called the bias. Wherever possible the grain of a fabric should run in the same direction on a quilt block and borders.

Grain lines These are arrows printed on templates which should be aligned with the fabric grain.

Inset seams or setting-in A patchwork technique whereby one patch (or block) is stitched into a V-shape formed by the joining of two other patches (or blocks).

Patch A small shaped piece of fabric used in the making of a patchwork pattern.

Patchwork The technique of stitching small pieces of fabric (patches) together to create a larger piece of fabric, usually forming a design.

Pieced quilt A quilt composed of patches.

Quilting Traditionally done by hand with running stitches, but for speed modern quilts are often stitched by machine. The stitches are sewn through the top, wadding and backing to hold the three layers together. Quilting stitches are usually worked in some form of design, but they can be random.

Quilting hoop Consists of two wooden circular or oval rings with a screw adjuster on the outer ring. It stabilises the quilt layers, helping to create an even tension.

Reducing glass Used for viewing the complete composition of a quilt at a glance. It works like a magnifier in reverse. A useful tool for checking fabric placement before piecing a quilt.

Rotary cutter A sharp circular blade attached to a handle for quick, accurate cutting. It is a device that can be used to cut several layers of fabric at one time. It must be used in conjunction with a self-healing cutting mat and a thick plastic ruler.

Rotary ruler A thick, clear plastic ruler marked with lines in imperial or metric measurements. Sometimes they also have diagonal lines indicating 45 and 60 degree angles. A rotary ruler is used as a guide when cutting out fabric pieces using a rotary cutter.

Sashing A piece or pieced sections of fabric interspaced between blocks.

Sashing posts When blocks have sashing between them the corner squares are known as sashing posts.

Selvedges Also known as selvages, these are the firmly woven edges down each side of a fabric length. Selvedges should be trimmed off before cutting out your fabric, as they are more liable to shrink when the fabric is washed.

Stitch-in-the-ditch or Ditch quilting Also known as quilting-in-the-ditch. The quilting stitches are worked along the actual seam lines to give a pieced quilt texture.

Template A pattern piece used as a guide for marking and cutting out fabric patches, or marking a quilting, or appliqué design. Usually made from plastic or strong card that can be reused many times. Templates for cutting fabric usually have marked grain lines which should be aligned with the fabric grain.

Threads One hundred percent cotton or cotton-covered polyester is best for hand and machine piecing. Choose a colour that matches your fabric. When sewing different colours and patterns together, choose a medium to light neutral colour, such as grey or ecru. Specialist quilting threads are available for hand and machine quilting.

Walking foot or Quilting foot This is a sewing machine foot with dual feed control. It is very helpful when quilting, as the fabric layers are fed evenly from the top and below, reducing the risk of slippage and puckering.

Yo-Yos A circle of fabric double the size of the finished puff is gathered up into a rosette shape.

Y-seams See Inset seams.

ACKNOWLEDGMENTS

These books are why I design fabrics: to create patchworks from the most recent fabrics that Brandon, Philip and I have designed before they hit the shops. Once the plan is set for each book, there is a small team of designers/makers that patiently sew, quilt and write the instructions for these books. Liza Prior Lucy is our trusted friend and loyal colleague, based in the US, along with fellow makers Bobbi Penniman, Sally Davis, Mira Mayer and Judy Baldwin, plus Judy Irish for quilting and, in the UK, Janet Haigh with Ilaria Padovani and Julie Harvey, plus Mary-Jane Hutchinson for quilting. Thanks to them all: were it not for them, these books would not be possible.*

Thanks, too, to Bundle Backhouse for taking on the enormous responsibility for technical editing and for her organizational skills at the Kaffe Fassett Studio; to Anne Wilson for her book layout skills and her attention to detail; and to Susan Berry of Berry & Co, our publishing consultant, for managing the *P & Q* books through their process to print.

Grateful thanks too to Simone Dinon and the charming people of the small colourful island of Burano, Venice, who provided the most spectacular backdrop for our collection of quilts for this, our 22nd *Patchwork & Quilting* book.

Many thanks to our ever-trusted friend and photographer, Debbie Patterson, who shares not only a similar eye but also our sense of humour. She puts up with Brandon's and my temperamental moods to arrive at just the magic we are aiming for. And, last but not least, to Brandon, who not only manages the Studio, and co-designs with me, but endures the pressures of our whirlwind shoots in various locations – so glad you hang in there, ensuring the output is consistently of quality.

* Midnight Diamonds (Sally Davis)
  Ocean Ripples (Ilaria Padovani)
  Shimmer Star (Liza Prior Lucy)
  Hot Steps (Ilaria Padovani)
  Cool Steps (Ilaria Padovani)
  Tawny Pinwheels (Judy Baldwin)
  Fruits of the Forest (Julie Harvey)
  Roman Tiles (Julie Harvey)
  Smouldering Stars (Julie Harvey)
  Dark Garden (Julie Harvey)
  Succulent (Julie Harvey)
  Honeycomb (Ilaria Padovani)
  Flaming Hell (Ilaria Padovani)
  Framed Log Cabin (Bobbi Penniman)
  Sun and Sea (Liza Prior Lucy)
  Geometric Snowballs (Julie Harvey)
  Green with Envy (Liza Prior Lucy)
  Diamond Carpet (Mira Mayer)
  Turkish Coffee (Liza Prior Lucy)

distributors and stockists

To find a retailer in the USA and Canada, please go to www.freespiritfabrics.com

For the following countries see contact information below:

AUSTRALIA
XLN Fabrics
2/21 Binney Rd
Kings Park
NSW 2148
www.xln.com.au
email: allanmurphy@xln.com.au

CHINA
Wan Mei Diy China
1458 GuMei Road, Room 502-14
Shanghai 201102
email: 12178550@qq.com

DENMARK
Industrial Textiles A/S
Engholm Parkvej 1
Alleroed 3450
www.indutex.dk
email: maria@indutex.dk

HONG KONG
See China

JAPAN
Kiyohara & Co Ltd
4-5-2 Minamikyuhoji-machi
Chuo-ku
Osaka 541-8506
www.kiyohara.co.jp

Yamachu-Mengyo Co Ltd
1-10-8 Edobori
Nishi-Ku,
Osaka 550-0002
www.yamachu-mengyo.co.jp

SOUTH KOREA
Elgatex
103 Park Palace 95
Naesoo-Dong, Jongno-gu
Seoul 110901
email: kennyel@unitel.co.kr

June Crafts
5022 B-BLD Dong Dea Mun Chain
28903 Jongno 6-GA
Jongno-gu,
Seoul
email: ityrhee@yahoo.com

MACAO
See China

NEW ZEALAND
Fabco Ltd
43 Lee Martin Road
Hamilton 3283
www.fabco.co.nz
email: melanie@fabco.co.nz

SINGAPORE
Sing Mui Heng
315 Outram
#13-03 Tan Boon Liat Building
email: mkt@singmuiheng.com

SOUTH AFRICA
Arthur Bales Pty Ltd
62 4th Avenue
Johannesburg 2103
www.arthurbales.co.za
email: nicci@arthurbales.co.za

SPAIN
Jose Rosas Taberner SA
Ave Mare de Deu de Montserrat 45
P I La Fonstanta
St Joan Despi Barcelona 8970
www.castelltort.com

TAIWAN
Long Teh Trading Co Ltd
No. 71 Hebei W. St
Tai Chung City 40669
email: Longteh.quilt@gmail.com

UK/EUROPE
Rhinetex BV
Maagdenburgstraat 24
ZC Deventer 7421
Netherlands
www.rhinetex.com
email: info@rhinetex.com

LOCATION OF THE ISLAND OF BURANO, VENICE